Lynch's enduring principles and practical insights will help people from all walks of life turn work and family obstacles into opportunities for success."

—Chet Edwards, former U.S. Congressman, Texas 17th District, 1991–2010

"General Lynch offers a rare and powerful perspective on leadership. Not only is he is a proven leader through his experiences as a U.S. Army general, but he is a natural leader from his innate understanding of and care for people."

—Jorgen Pedersen, president and CEO, RE2, Inc.

"Rick personifies what leadership is all about. He has a way of communicating how to lead through strength, compassion, and most of all integrity! No matter if you lead a corporation, a small business, a nonprofit, or an academic institution, Rick's principles will guide you to success."

—Doug Harward, CEO and founder, TrainingIndustry.com

"Hard-hitting, straightforward Rick Lynch captures a lifetime of lessons learned from a very distinguished military career—invaluable for corporate and military leaders alike."

—Gen. (Ret.) Ben Griffin, U.S. Army

"With boldness and candor, Rick Lynch relates his own experiences from a distinguished U.S. Army career to illustrate essential leadership principles for all of us. General Lynch is an authentic American hero, yet he writes with a common touch. He demonstrates a deep understanding of how to be a leader and to live a full, balanced life."

—James D. Spaniolo, president, University of Texas at Arlington

"Leadership is what we desperately need, yet it's not an innate trait. Fortunately, it can be learned, and we have Lt. Gen. Rick Lynch to teach us. From the heartland of America to the distant ramparts of Iraq, Lynch knows the importance of leadership and wants to share his gift with others. This book is more than the fascinating journey of an accomplished American patriot. It is a guide for all of us on how to lead and how to live."

—Dr. J. D. Crouch II, former assistant to the president and deputy national security advisor

"I personally have experienced the wonderful impact of Rick and these stories. He will touch all of your emotions. Most important,

ADAPT OR DIE

BATTLE-TESTED
PRINCIPLES FOR LEADERS

U.S. ARMY COMMANDER OF THE THIRD INFANTRY
DIVISION DURING THE "SURGE" IN IRAQ

LT GEN (RET) RICK LYNCH

with MARK DAGOSTINO

"'Change, adapt, and find new opportunities.' That is how Rick Lynch commanded in Iraq during the surge. But it could be any of us leaders anywhere: We all have to adapt. This is a superb book on leadership written by a thoughtful, courageous, and authentic leader himself. As wise, practical, and inspiring as any I have ever seen."

—Gen. (Ret.) Fred M. Franks, U.S. Army

"General Lynch's book *Adapt or Die* is a wonderful reflection of the importance of truly caring for people in a very emotional and deeply connected way. I have worked with Rick in helping take care of our soldiers and their families during these difficult times, and the leadership principles listed in this book are an invaluable guide on how to accomplish that goal. Those principles apply not only in the military, but also in corporate America, in academia, and even in the entertainment industry."

—Gary Sinise, actor and founder of the Gary Sinise Foundation

"General Lynch is a great American hero. He's led our troops in battle and he's managed the bases for thousands of military families around the world. He's got insights into leadership and taking care of people that are great lessons for leaders of any organization. He makes a compelling case for leaders to constantly improve and adapt their organizations; it's really all about people. Lynch's mantra of 'touching lives and making a difference' should speak to leaders of all types of organizations. A must-read for any student of leaders."

—Craig Boyan, president and COO, H-E-B

"Three Cheers for *Adapt or Die*! General Lynch shows us that leadership is not just a matter of the head, but of the heart; not just an acquired skill, but a gift bestowed. With accuracy, detail, and precision, Ricky Lynch hands his reader a magnifying glass, allowing us to peer upon the essential qualities of a caring, effective, passionate, and successful leader."

—Rev. Dr. Russell J. Levenson Jr., Rector, St. Martin's
Episcopal Church, Houston, Texas

"This book deserves a place on the shelf of contemporary leadership tomes. A personal tour through an exciting life as a soldier, it will provoke an interesting self-analysis in those who have led or want to lead."

—Lt. Gen. (Ret.) Walter F. Ulmer Jr., U.S. Army
former president and CEO, Center for Creative Leadership

"*Adapt or Die* is an inspiring story of the lessons learned about faith, life, and leadership from one of America's great soldiers. General

you will leave feeling more prepared and motivated to lead yourself, your team, and your organization."

—Al Triunfo, vice president, sales and operations, MEDA Pharmaceuticals

"*Adapt or Die* is an invaluable addition to a leadership library and can truly help people who strive to be leaders in the godly way. General Lynch shows us how he leaned on God throughout his career, especially in difficult circumstances, and how that relationship was a source of strength for him. I wish I could have read this book forty years ago."

—Dan Wallrath, president/founder, Operation Finally Home

"This book deserves a look as an example of how one aggressive general officer sees his profession, himself, and his responsibilities. It is a candid, straightforward review of the challenge and response of a military leader in today's complex environment."

—Brig. Gen. (Ret.) John C. (Doc) Bahnsen, U.S. Army

"General Lynch gives pragmatic examples of how investing in and trusting your employees can and does lead to significant productivity and morale changes. *Adapt or Die* is a must-read for anyone who has been blessed with people responsibility or for those who aspire to lead effectively."

—Bob Jansen, president and CEO, Zensights

"Managers, pastors, military leaders, educators, and anyone seeking to lead well will find great help in the pages of this book. General Lynch has earned the right to be heard, and listening to his instruction and stories will lock fresh new leadership lessons in your heart."

—Rev. Kevin G. Harney, pastor, leadership trainer, and author of *Reckless Faith* and *The Organic Outreach Series*

"An inspiring book by one of our nation's premier strategic and spiritual leaders. Having achieved success as a military professional at every level of the army's organizational structure, General Rick Lynch's valuable and practical leadership principles captured in this volume should be required reading for any organization's entire management team—no matter the position or level. Quite simply, this might be one of the most positive, candid, and encouraging books I've read on leadership in recent years! Truly an invaluable resource for those wanting to take their effectiveness as a great, adaptive leader to the next level."

—Chaplain Maj. Gen. (Ret.) Doug Carver, U.S. Army

To Rick
Thanks for all you do!

ADAPT
OR DIE

Take care T God bless

ADAPT OR DIE

BATTLE-TESTED PRINCIPLES FOR LEADERS

LT GEN (RET) RICK LYNCH
WITH MARK DAGOSTINO

BakerBooks
a division of Baker Publishing Group
Grand Rapids, Michigan

© 2013 by Lt. Gen. (Ret.) Rick Lynch

Published by Baker Books
a division of Baker Publishing Group
P.O. Box 6287, Grand Rapids, MI 49516-6287
www.bakerbooks.com

Paperback edition published 2015
ISBN 978-0-8010-1844-2

Printed in the United States of America

The Library of Congress has cataloged the original edition as follows:
Lynch, Rick.
    Adapt or die : leadership principles from an American general / Lt. Gen. (Ret.) Rick
Lynch, with Mark Dagostino.
        pages cm
    Summary: "The Army general who successfully led the surge in Iraq shares stories and lessons from the front lines, demonstrating the necessity for leaders to learn the art of adaptation in an ever-changing world"—Provided by publisher.
    ISBN 978-0-8010-1565-6 (cloth : alk. paper)
    1. Leadership. 2. Command of troops—Case studies. 3. Change (Psychology)
4. Spiritual life. I. Dagostino, Mark. II. Title.
HM1261.L96 2013
303.3′4—dc23   2013023275

Author is represented by Alive Communications, Inc.

15   16   17   18   19   20   21   7   6   5   4   3   2   1

To Sarah,
for all of your love and support through the years

Contents

Contents

Introduction

If you picked up this book, chances are pretty good that you've made up your mind: You want to be a leader. Or maybe you're already a leader and you want to be a better leader. A stronger leader. Either way, that's a very good thing.

We need more leaders. True leaders. Leaders who know what it means to "lead" and not just "manage."

America's got problems. Our governments (both national and local), our businesses (both big and small), our education systems (both private and public), even our churches and community organizations are facing budget cuts and shortfalls, global competition, shifting demographics, loss of morale and of moral direction, and a never-ending series of rapidly changing technological challenges that seem almost too big to bear. Yet all of this can be solved. I believe the solution to almost every problem we face is strong leadership—leadership built on the ability to adapt.

Adaptation, as history shows us, is the key to survival not only in business or out on the battlefield, but in life. The phrase "Adapt or die" exists for a reason, and the best leaders, the strongest leaders, live by it.

The world moves fast today—faster than a lot of seemingly capable leaders and even some well-oiled machines and top-notch organizations can handle. But true leaders know how to adapt and how to get those around them to adapt to any situation.

Think you've got what it takes to be that kind of a leader? I think you do. I believe in the power of individuals to change their circumstances, to change their environment, to change the course of their home life and workplaces, and to change for the better. You have the strength it takes to do that, using the tools that God blessed you with. The question is whether you have the belief that you have what it takes to get it done, and whether you can recognize how to use the tools you've been given.

My aim in writing this book is to help you do just that.

The thing is, once you know your foundation, once you have your guiding principles in place, leading is basically a matter of digging deep and choosing to do the right thing—no matter how big or how small the challenges before you may be.

So what are those challenges? After thirty-five years in the army, leading groups of American heroes as small as one hundred soldiers and as large as 120,000 civilian employees, chances are I've not only faced it, but survived it, overcome it, and come out the other side better for it. In fact, no matter how big your challenges might seem, I bet I've got a story that'll help put it all into perspective for you.

Got a budget to trim? I was required to trim $5 billion from one of my budgets over a two-year period without cutting back on any of the services we were tasked to deliver. Facing a tough negotiation? In Iraq, I sat across the negotiating table from sixteen heavily armed Sunni insurgents who were hell-bent on killing me, with no one but a translator to back me up on my side of the table—and won. How did I do that? The same way I've adapted and pushed through every decision and struggle in my life: by seeing opportunities instead of obstacles; by acting as an engaged leader; by standing up as a lifestyle evangelist who leads not just with words, but by example; and by knowing my priorities and standing on a solid foundation that allows me—and therefore, those around me—to adapt and persevere with resilience.

It took me a lifetime to learn how to master those principles. In the pages of this book, I'll share stories and examples from a variety of points in my life and career in the hopes that you'll learn a little faster than I did, and start leading with courage and conviction right away, no matter what challenges come your way.

In life and work, it's almost a certainty that you'll face challenges you don't see coming. In fact, one of the toughest foes to ever face me down in my entire career was a young woman—an army wife—who stopped me on the street with tears in her eyes three days after I took over command at Fort Hood, Texas, the largest army base in the free world.

"You generals are lying to us!" she said to me.

I was taken aback. "Ma'am, I don't understand," I said.

"You tell us that you're bringing our husbands home between deployments. You say it, but you don't mean it. Here at Fort Hood, my husband comes home every night after our kids go to bed. He's always working weekends," she said. "Just keep him. You're teasing my family. My kids understand why Daddy's gone when he's in Iraq or Afghanistan, but they don't understand why they never get to see him when he's right here in Texas."

A manager might hear a complaint like this, show some sympathy, and basically go back to whatever he or she was doing before. "Tough," might be the internal response. "There's work to be done and our soldiers are here to do it." But neglect and denial just aren't my style. What this young woman was telling me was something that had been churning in my gut for some time: We as the army hadn't done enough to adapt our systems, schedules, and routines back home to a war that was now stretching toward a decade in length. The war, with its multiple back-to-back deployments, was taxing our soldiers and their families to the brink. We knew it, but we weren't doing enough about it. We needed to adapt to this new reality before the whole system simply died under our watch.

As a leader, I realized it wasn't anyone else's responsibility. It was my responsibility to do something about it, and to do something about it right away.

That very day, I demanded that all 63,000 soldiers at Fort Hood be home by 6:00 to eat dinner with their families. It's a demand I would enforce from that day forward. Five days a week. I also insisted that every soldier and officer (the equivalents of "supervisors" and "bosses" in my organization) leave work at 3 p.m. on Thursdays for mandatory family time—to join in afternoon ball games and bonding activities that had been set up prior to my taking over Fort Hood, but which were never truly enforced. I also declared that no soldier would be allowed to work weekends without my personal approval. (And guess how many soldiers were willing to seek approval from a general for *that*?)

I know there are CEOs all across the country laughing at the very idea of ever demanding that their employees leave early, shaking their heads at the ridiculous notion that a workday could end at 3 p.m. even one day a week without destroying productivity.

I'm here to tell you CEOs that you're just plain wrong.

This sweeping order not only resulted in a significant drop in incidences of domestic violence, divorce, and failed relationships, but Fort Hood, which held the dubious distinction of having the highest suicide rate of any base in the army, exhibited the *lowest* suicide rates in the army just a year later.

By guiding people toward better balance in their lives, morale went up. Productivity went up. We didn't lose anything. In fact, just the opposite. Work got done and then some. Our soldiers became more efficient, more productive, more effective during the course of the day, and we all enjoyed the benefits. Traffic accidents, which were rampant—we had traffic fatalities every fifteen to twenty days on base—nearly disappeared. At one point we went 245 days without a single fatality, thanks to a broad spectrum of directives I put into place to improve work/life balance, and by insisting that platoon leaders (my "middle management" as it were) pay more attention to the personal safety of our soldiers at every level.

It's a documented example of "family first" policies that made a major difference in a lot of people's lives, including my own. I walked the walk. If I told my soldiers to be home for dinner by six

16

o'clock, you'd better believe I was home for dinner by six myself. If I told them to leave at three o'clock on Thursdays, I left at three on Thursdays. And if I said, "We're not working on weekends," I wouldn't work on weekends. Period.

I did find myself getting up at four in the morning to work two and a half hours before heading into the office most days because I didn't want to sacrifice the time with my family the night before. So you do have to work hard as a leader—harder than anyone else on your team at times—but you don't have to sacrifice your family or anyone else's family time in order to do that.

My bold move resonated across the entire army, and a long-entrenched culture began to change almost overnight. In 2009, the *Austin American Statesmen* wrote an article dubbing me "The Family First General," and I couldn't have been more proud.

You might be asking yourself, *What on earth does that story have to do with leading "my company" or "my department" or "my university" or "my organization"?* It has to do with treating your subordinates, your work force, your team—the individual members of whatever group it is that you're tasked with leading—as if they were your very own children. And that may sound like a lot of soft talk coming from a three-star general, but I hope you'll see by the end of this book that it's actually just about the toughest talk I could lay on you. I hope you'll learn that the only way you're going to get ahead, the only way you're going to get on course, the only way you're going to move your company forward, and the only way to move this country forward—in education, in business, in politics, in everything—is to live by one very important rule: Treat your people well, and they'll treat you well in return. I've followed that rule from life-or-death situations on the battlefield to nine-to-five obligations back home, and the results have always, always been positive.

Of the many examples of my personal leadership style I'll share in this book, one tenet that undergirds everything is that our people are our most important resource. If we don't take care of them, they won't have the ability to adapt. And what happens when you don't adapt? That's right. You die. Your organization dies. Your government dies. Your business dies. On the battlefield, your people themselves will die. Today in America, if we don't take care of our people first and lead them through the example of strong leadership, I'm afraid the very spirit that keeps this country thriving is going to die, too.

I don't mean to sound overly dramatic here, but in life, you worry about the things you love. And I love our nation. We've got some big problems, and I don't see a way out of these problems without strong leadership on our side.

Our leaders have to know that our people are what matter. When leaders forget that, I believe it is to our great peril.

I ask that you keep this in mind as we forge ahead. It's at the root of everything I have ever done as a leader. Everything I hope that you, the leaders of today and the leaders of tomorrow, will embrace for the sake of us all.

PART 1

OPPORTUNITIES, NOT OBSTACLES

Have I not commanded you? Be strong and courageous. Do not be afraid; do not be discouraged, for the Lord your God will be with you wherever you go.

Joshua 1:9

Obstacles are a part of life, and great leaders see obstacles for what they really are: opportunities. Nurturing your ability to see through obstacles is one key to becoming a great leader. The fact is, if you're not facing obstacles in your life and work, if you find yourself gliding along in your comfort zone all the time, you're probably working in the wrong place. Push harder. Look for opportunities to work outside your comfort zone. Face obstacles head on, find the strength to push through them, and you'll find that the rewards on the other side are almost always greater than you could have expected. It takes some strength and a whole lot of faith to push through sometimes. But do you know what it all comes down to? Your attitude. It's up to you to choose: Is this obstacle the thing that'll do you in? That'll shut you down? That'll stop you dead in your tracks? Or is this obstacle simply a challenge that's going to cause you to grow and learn and become better at whatever it is you do?

I choose to see opportunities, not obstacles. What do you choose to see?

1

No Money

Growing up as a kid in Hamilton, Ohio, potato soup was the high-light meal of my week.

Needless to say, my family had no money.

Our household included not only me, my mom, my dad, and my younger brother, but since Dad had been married previously, I had two half brothers who were there sometimes as well—and all together we rarely had a nickel between us.

Like a lot of other parents in our small city, Mom and Dad both worked shift work at the paper mill: seven to three, three to eleven, or eleven to seven, day in and day out, and despite working all those hours, neither of them brought home much of a paycheck. They provided for the family as best they could. I'm not complaining. I'm eternally grateful for their hard work, but there was simply nothing left over at the end of the week. That posed certain challenges. It didn't matter that things cost less then. It didn't matter that my parents could give me a dollar to run to the store for a half gallon of milk, a loaf of bread, and a pack of cigarettes, and I'd bring 'em back change. We were still barely scraping by.

It was clear to me by the age of thirteen that if I wanted to have nice school clothes or have my own transportation or be able to go to McDonald's with my buddies, Mom and Dad weren't going to hand me a ten-dollar bill and say, "Go have a nice time."

So at thirteen I went looking for work.

That was a pretty big turning point and a springboard into many life lessons learned. Even before that I was ambitious. I worked on my cousin's dairy farm in Indiana, pulling in sixty cents an hour as a kid. But the first real job I found as a teenager was painting houses. There was a guy who worked with Mom at the paper mill who had a side business painting houses, inside and outside. So I threw myself into it and started putting money away for the things I wanted.

Over the next few years I migrated from that to the restaurant business. I was a busboy and then a grill cook—like a lot of kids. And by the time I was a senior in high school I was working as the assistant manager of a pet store in Hamilton.

Nobody ever said, "Hey, Rick, you gotta get a job." It was just clear to me that if I didn't get a job, I wasn't going to have what I wanted. And if I give my parents credit for anything, especially my mom, it's instilling this profound work ethic: Working hard is the right thing to do, and if you ever find yourself not working hard, then you're probably not in the right position.

There are people in life (and a lot of people in today's America) who would look at my thirteen-year-old self and see the whole situation as something negative. As if it were a burden that I had to get a job. But I didn't see it that way then, and I certainly don't see it that way now. The fact that my parents didn't have money and didn't hand me everything I wanted wasn't an obstacle. It was an opportunity—an opportunity of a lifetime, because it set me up for a lifetime of success.

When I got my first job, I got my first sense of independence. For the first time in my life I wasn't relying on my mom or dad. I had my own money. I could buy my own clothes. I could go to McDonald's whenever I wanted without relying on anyone else's handouts. And when I turned sixteen I bought my own motorcycle: a Yamaha 175

Enduro. That's how I got back and forth to school, and it's also how I got back and forth to work in the restaurant business.

Many years later, when I became a lieutenant in the army, I read an article on career development that pointed to one very important trait of success: Do every job superbly. I already knew that firsthand because of my early work experience as a teenager, and because it was something my mom taught me. Regardless of whether you're a house painter, a dishwasher, a grill cook, or a lieutenant, do the best job you can and you'll always be successful, Mom used to tell me. Of course, the article also said that another aspect of success is to make sure people know that you're doing a good job: Be visible and widely known! That would get easier for me over time. I wasn't much of a people person early on. I was more of an introvert. But in time I would grow to enjoy talking to people and getting to know everyone, no matter where I worked.

Seeing opportunities instead of obstacles is about having the right mind-set. For me, beginning at age thirteen, part of that was a realization that your current set in life does not have to be permanent. You have a choice, and you can change whatever it is that's holding you back. You can make those changes with a positive attitude, and as a result of that positive attitude you can work through it. If you don't do that—and unfortunately I see this all the time—you can fall into a state of resignation: "It is what it is. It ain't gonna get any better than this." Think of the state of the nation these days, and this overwhelming sense of resignation that's swept across America. People talk as if everything just is what it is: Unemployment is the way it is, the deficit's the way it is, governmental paralysis is the way it is, and there's nothing we can do about any of it.

That's letting the obstacle blur the opportunity.

I go back to Joshua 1:9 all the time: "Do not be afraid; do not be discouraged." That conviction and determined spirit alone gives me the strength and courage to plow on today. But I didn't have the Bible and those teachings in my life when I was thirteen years old. I didn't get that until I started going to church almost twenty years later. So where did I get that conviction and spirit from?

I think I got it from my mom. I love my dad, but he wasn't the nurturer. He was the guy with the belt. Mom was the nurturer: caring and loving, with an infectious laugh. Her name was Dorothy, but everyone called her Dotie. It was a fitting nickname because, in fact, she doted on my brother and me all the time. She doted on us so much that it was a major bone of contention between her and my dad. He would always complain that she was "trying to spoil those kids." Maybe she *was* trying to spoil us, by spending more time with us. Every year she would go into debt to buy us Christmas presents, and then we'd see her work even harder just to pay off that debt. Because of that extra time and affection she showed, she has proven to be the most influential person in our lives.

I never saw my mom complain. The lot in life that she had was good enough for her—even if she knew it wasn't good enough for my brother or me. She wanted more for us, and she made that clear. To be fair, so did my dad.

My father, Calvin, graduated from the seventh grade, and that's as far as he got in school because he didn't think he needed any more than that. Mom graduated from the eleventh grade, so neither one of them were high school graduates. But Mom was the gal who always advocated that we needed to get straight A's if we wanted to get ahead in life. She pushed us in her kind and gentle fashion. Dad, on the other hand—if you didn't get straight A's, you had some explaining to do when you got home. It was that level of discipline with him: Even though he only had a seventh-grade education, he wouldn't have tolerated anything but the best from my brother and me.

It's funny to think about, but the roots of your upbringing run deep. There is something that happened there in Hamilton, Ohio, in all of those lessons and all of that pushing from my parents during my formative years that really carried me to where I am today. There was something in all of it that gave me the foundation of optimism—this steadfast belief that I could overcome obstacles and turn them into opportunities, every time.

Colin Powell says, "Optimism is a combat multiplier." I believe that's true. When you look at lists of famous people's quotations, especially famous leaders, you see a lot about optimism. Abraham Lincoln said, "A man is about as happy as he makes his mind up to be." I believe that's true, too.

As you're confronted with difficult circumstances, your outlook is everything. Your outlook is going to help you overcome the obstacles and turn them into opportunities. Every time. But you need to have a positive attitude—otherwise you risk shutting down. Otherwise you miss seeing the opportunity that's right there in front of you, or asking for advice that just might lead you to an opportunity you never knew existed.

2

Beast Barracks

Getting over the "no-money" obstacle was pretty easy as a teen. I found work. I made money. Problem solved. But I was a junior in high school when that obstacle grew into a problem that I thought was wholly insurmountable: There was no way that my parents could ever afford to send me to college, and even though I was working, I knew in my heart there was no way I could ever afford to pay a bill as big as college tuition.

I was a good student. My parents saw to that, and I saw to it. I got all A's. It wasn't like I was a genius or something. I just worked hard. I worked hard at whatever I did, be it schoolwork or house painting. But what good would that do me if I couldn't go to college? If I couldn't find a way to pay for school, I thought, I might wind up working at the paper mill just like my parents, and I knew I didn't want to do that.

How on earth could a kid go to college if he didn't have a way to pay for it?

Since my parents didn't have an answer, and my peers didn't have an answer, and I couldn't seem to come up with an answer myself, I went to see the guidance counselor at my high school. "Ma'am,"

I said, "I'm getting all A's, as you well know. I'm on the honor roll here, I'm in the National Honor Society, but my parents can't afford to send me to college. Is there any way I can still go to school?"

Her response? "How about a military academy?" I had no idea what a military academy was, so I said, "What's that?" Her answer just about blew my mind: "Well, that's a place where they *pay you* to go to school."

No one had ever told me that such a place existed! Ever since the inkling of an idea of a college education was put into my head, I had been told that it was something that cost a whole lot of money. All it took was asking the right question to the right person with the right knowledge, and the whole notion that college wasn't affordable was no longer a concern. "Okay!" I said. "Let's try that!"

So basically, the fact that I didn't have any money suddenly turned into another amazing opportunity: Not only could I still go to school, but there were schools out there that would pay me to go! Talk about a win-win situation.

Of course, my interest in going to a military academy had nothing to do with an aspiration to join the military.

My dad was a private E1 in 1945 when he was drafted into the army—that's the lowest rank on the totem pole, so to speak—and he was a private E1 when he was kicked out of the army two years later, in 1947. He was the world's worst soldier, a fact he's very proud of to this day. So the inspiration certainly didn't come from him.

To tell the truth, I didn't really think a whole lot about the military part of the equation. All I saw was the possibility of my getting a free college education, and the unbelievably big bonus of getting paid for the chance to go get it.

That guidance counselor's advice marked a significant moment in my life, that's for sure. She also said I should look at Reserve Officer Training Corps (ROTC) scholarships to non-military schools because they could provide for a four-year education as well. That was a whole other way to get the education I desired with no money out of my own pocket. I could hardly believe it! So I applied for and received a four-year ROTC scholarship, and wound up applying to ten different schools that would've taken it. I only went to visit one, though: Ohio State. That school seemed really appealing, and I thought in my heart that's where I was going to go and put that scholarship to good use. But this was 1972. If you recall, in 1972, people didn't like the United States military very much. On the heels of Vietnam and the incident at Kent State, I stepped foot onto the campus in Columbus and quickly realized that if I went there in uniform, I was sure to be a persona non grata. So I said to myself, "I might as well go to the military academy where everybody's the same and nobody's throwing stuff at you!" The military academy was the clear choice.

I went through the application process to both West Point and Annapolis. I got my West Point acceptance on a Tuesday and my Annapolis acceptance on a Wednesday. The only reason I chose West Point was that the acceptance letter came in first. The postman determined my fate.

"West Point? Are you crazy?!" my dad said when I told him that I was accepted there. "That's the army!"

By that point there was no way he could have deterred me. My independence had pretty much been established. So I ignored his warnings about how tough it would be and how much I would hate it, and I packed my bags with no idea what lay ahead.

Money was still an issue of course. I had to buy a pair of black shoes before they'd let me step foot onto that campus. And I had to have $300 set aside in order to open the account where the army would deposit my pay while I was in school. Luckily my grandmother loaned me the money for both. There's nothing like family to back you up when you're first stepping foot into the world.

I still remember vividly the sight of Coco, our family poodle, looking out the door after me as I got into the car and drove off to the airport. I was scared to death that day. I had no idea what I was getting into. Everything I was fixing to do was going to be a first for me. I cried when the car pulled away from the house, and I cried when I got on the plane. This young green kid flew to New York City all by himself, and I cried when the plane landed! I had rarely been out of the state of Ohio, and there I was plopped in that sprawling metropolis with no one to guide me. I was literally the country boy in the big city. All the new recruits had to stay at a particular hotel, and after I checked in, I basically spent the night by myself. I'm an introvert by nature, and I was particularly introverted early in my adult life, so it was very difficult for me to talk to strangers or to make new friends. I remember going to see a James Bond movie instead of trying to get to know anyone.

It was July 2, 1973.

Representatives from West Point came and picked us all up the next morning and drove us down to that beautiful high-ground campus overlooking the Hudson River. But as soon as we got off the bus, the yelling, screaming, harassment, and drills began. I vividly remember thinking that everything at West Point was uphill, because they made you run all the time and it seemed like everywhere you ran was uphill—there wasn't a downhill stretch to be found!

Even something as simple as eating dinner was a challenge. The way West Point is organized, the mess hall has these ten-man tables. The upperclassmen are all at the head of the table, and at the foot are three plebes (that's what freshman were called). One plebe is designated the "cold beverage corporal." He's required to know what everybody wants to drink. One is the dessert cutter. And one guy is there just to take all the wrath of the upperclassmen. The long and short of it was that those three plebes—of which I was one—never got a chance to eat. I would leave that mess hall just about starving every single day.

If you've ever seen a movie depicting the sort of harassment that goes on in these places, you have some idea of what I'm talking about here. But believe me, you have no idea what it feels like to be chastised and yelled and screamed at for hours and hours for days on end until it actually happens to you. And it is miserable.

There's a name for this six-week indoctrination period at West Point. They call it Beast Barracks, and there couldn't be a more fitting name. I think I went in weighing 175 pounds, and six weeks later I was down to 145. And remember, I had no idea what I was getting into before I got there. I hadn't prepared for that experience at all. I only went there because I couldn't afford to go to any other college. Nobody had prepared me for this extreme entry into adulthood.

Three weeks into it I felt defeated. I thought, *This is not going to work for me.* I was completely overwhelmed.

I called my dad and said, "You were right. I can't do this. The army's not for me. I'm coming home."

Guess what my dad's reply was?

"Oh yeah?" he said. "Where are you gonna sleep?"

Tough love.

I didn't appreciate it much at the time, as you might imagine. But that tough love was exactly what I needed in that moment. The fact is, the army wanted to break me down. And they had. They did a good job! They wanted to break me down to build me up; instill a discipline that would be lifelong and unforgettable. We don't do that so much anymore in the army because, candidly, that was just pure, unadulterated harassment. We don't want our officers to treat their subordinates that poorly in the field, so why were we treating them like that at the academy? But good, bad, or indifferent, Beast Barracks was a part of what it took to get to the glorious education that awaited me on the other side. Only I was so broken down that I nearly succumbed to the obstacle, right there. I nearly gave in. I was overwhelmed by the negativity of it all. I couldn't see the bigger picture, couldn't see the opportunity that getting through this harassment and pain and suffering was going to bring my way. I needed my dad's tough love, his refusal to let me quit, in order to get through it.

"You started it—you're going to finish it." That was his message. So I hung up the phone and went back to Beast Barracks. After another three weeks of hell, it was over. Then it started to feel more like school—a really good school with fantastic teachers, and students who wanted to succeed. Sophomore year was called our Yearling Year, and by the time I was halfway through it, I started to hit my stride. I went back to what I knew: Hard work yields results. I did all of the things that cadets were supposed to be doing. I saw the rewards of that hard work in my grades. I became a Star Man, which meant I was in the top 5 percent of my class. I was also selected to command one of four regiments at the school. Becoming a regimental commander is one of the highest achievements at the academy! And before long, I found myself truly enjoying my time at West Point.

If I had given up, if I had given in to the obstacles they threw at me in those first six weeks, I never would have found that sense of enjoyment. I never would have discovered the passion for leadership that would launch me into a thirty-five-year career. It was a great lesson in the power of commitment.

Applying that sort of tough love to myself is something that would take years to master. Heck, I still haven't mastered it! There have been plenty of other times in my career when I wanted to quit—I'll talk about those in upcoming chapters. But not giving in, not giving up, and following through until you get to the other side of the challenge are important first steps in learning how to lead—not to mention learning how to adapt and move forward when the going gets tough.

Resist the urge to quit—and do your best to instill that resistance in those working under you. You won't regret it. There's opportunity in the obstacle. Every time. You just have to work a little harder to see it.

—————— REMINDER ——————

FOCUS ON OPPORTUNITIES, NOT OBSTACLES.

"It can be done!"

3

Speak Up!

I graduated from West Point as an engineer officer. In broad terms, the army defines an engineer officer as someone who provides support for all of the engineering duties in the army. That support could come in the form of construction (roads, bases, bridges), conducting reconnaissance and demolition duties, or in training the force with new engineering technologies. Any way you look at it, it was all about one word: support. Engineers are always answering to someone else. Engineers are always playing a supporting role. And I knew very early on that wasn't the role I wanted to play. But this was the army. You do what you're told. You follow orders. So I settled in to my new home in Fort Hood, Texas—the largest army base in the free world—and got to working.

A couple of years into this new career of mine, the army looked at what a hard worker I was and decided to promote me. They made me a first lieutenant, appointing me the adjutant for the Seventeenth Engineer Battalion. That may sound like a good thing on paper, but to put it bluntly, the job sucked. I was the perpetual middleman, the clean-up guy, the go-to secretary who solved everybody else's problems. I would show up to work with an agenda, and within two minutes the phone would ring and that entire agenda would be blown to bits. Every day I wound up faced with somebody else's crisis and had to spend all day chasing my tail trying to deal with that crisis.

I got so fed up, I finally went to the battalion commander and told him straight up, "I'm going to have to resign my commission. This is not what I want to do."

What *did* I want to do? I wanted to lead. I wanted to be a company commander. I knew I had what it took to be a leader, and yet the army was burying me in this job I couldn't stand. I was so fed up with the whole thing, I was fully prepared to quit and go find another career.

My battalion commander sensed just how serious I was, and since he didn't want to see me leave, he suggested I try something else. "How about you go interview to be Doc Bahnsen's aide?" he said.

Doc Bahnsen was a legend. He was serving as the one-star assistant division commander of the Second Armored Division at the time. But it's his history that made soldiers stand a little taller when he walked into a room. This is a guy they wrote a book about with the rather bold title, *American Warrior*. He's a man who won a distinguished service cross and five silver stars in Vietnam, who commanded a cavalry squadron when he was just a major—you're supposed to be a lieutenant colonel to do that. He was about as intimidating as a guy could be, but he seemed like the kind of leader I could learn from. *Being an aide is better than being the adjutant,* I thought, so I decided to interview, even though I still had a great big chip on my shoulder.

I walked into Bahnsen's office. "Lieutenant Lynch reporting," I said.

He cut to the chase: "What are you here for, Lieutenant?"

"Sir, I'm here to interview to be your aide."

"Why do you want to be my aide?" he asked.

Here's where I decided to show a little courage, and perhaps a bit of brash stupidity. "I don't want to be your aide," I told him. "I just don't want to be the adjutant anymore. What I really want to be is a company commander."

It's hard to describe just how angry General Bahnsen turned in that moment. Nobody talked to Doc Bahnsen that way. Nobody! Let alone some lowly lieutenant. "Get out of my office!" he yelled.

Well . . . that's that, I figured. *My career is over.*

As I made the long walk back from division headquarters to battalion headquarters, I started thinking seriously about what I could do to make a living after I left the army. I was absolutely positive I had just thrown any chance of staying in the army right out the proverbial window.

I couldn't have been more wrong.

While I was busy beating myself up for my behavior, General Bahnsen picked up a phone and called my battalion commander—not to have me punished, but to give him an order that would change my role in the army from that day forward. An order that would change everything for me, which my rather dumbfounded battalion commander would relay to me the moment I stepped foot back into his office.

You know what Doc Bahnsen ordered the battalion commander to do after our short, blunt, rather heated meeting? "Make Lynch a company commander."

I was shocked! "Why would he do that?" I asked.

And the battalion commander told me exactly what Bahnsen told him: "Anybody with that much fire and passion deserves to be a company commander."

I signed for my first company the next day. In a matter of seconds, Doc Bahnsen made me the leader I wanted to be all along. All because I spoke up and spoke my mind.

If that event had not taken place, I would not be where I am today.

Speak From the Heart

Sometimes you have to exhibit the moral courage, the personal courage to do what you think is right, and to *say* what you think is right— even if you run the risk of getting into some trouble for saying it.

If you're not happy with your circumstances, don't just accept them—go out there and try to change them.

Far too often people have a sense of resignation: *This is my lot in life and it's as good as it's going to get, and that's it.* You cannot do that. You can't. Doc Bahnsen saw something in me because of what

I did in his office. And two years later, after I commanded that company he put me in charge of for two full years, I reported to General Bahnsen's office once again—this time as a captain.

"What are you here for, Lynch?" he asked.

"Sir, I've commanded my company now for two years. I've been at Fort Hood for four and a half years even though it's normally only a three-year tour, and the army's saying I've got to go take another posting somewhere else."

That's just the way things work in the army. They move you around. They change your position. That's the rule. And the thing a lot of strong leaders know is that rules don't always apply to every individual in an organization. Sometimes rules have to be broken, or at least bent, in service to a greater good.

Bahnsen had grown to like me in those last two years.

He said, "You're not leaving here. I'm going to put you in another company."

I watched him make one phone call after another until he finally got hold of the two-star general and got permission for me to stay.

So I signed to take the reins of my second company and wound up staying at Fort Hood, Texas, for an unprecedented six years—all because a guy like Doc Bahnsen said, "I'm not going to take 'no' for an answer. I know what's right for this guy. He needs to be a company commander again, so we're going to allow him to command for three continuous years."

Just so you understand what a bending of the rules that was, a company commander only served an average of twelve months total in that position back at that time in the army. So Bahnsen's actions tripled my time in that role.

And it all traces back to my bold but truthful words: "I don't want to be your aide." As I look back on that moment, I don't think it was a case of my being young and stupid. Not at all. I see it as something that was part and parcel of my desire to become a leader: the ability to show professional, personal, and moral courage.

I think that's how Doc Bahnsen saw it, too. And that was a valuable lesson: If you find yourself in an uncomfortable circumstance, don't just throw up your hands and say, "It is what it is." Figure out a way to work your way out of it. You don't have to be rude to do it, but you can state your mind in a thoughtful, tactful fashion. However you do it, it's certainly better than just throwing up your hands because nobody's listening. You've got to keep trying. You've got to find the right person to talk to. I had been telling everyone what I wanted to do all along. I had been saying, continuously, to anyone who would listen, that I wanted to be a company commander.

General Doc Bahnsen turned out to be the guy who was not only willing to listen, but also willing to take action to do something about it.

If I hadn't spoken my mind, if I hadn't told him what I really wanted to do, there is just no way I would have gotten what I wanted. If I hadn't spoken up, I never would have found the opportunity that existed in the obstacle of that terrible job the army had stuck me with. Turns out, having that awful job of adjutant drove me to bold action—to taking one big and necessary step toward being the leader I wanted to be.

Looking back on that period, what I really learned by doing and watching was that in order to be a successful company commander, I needed to be aggressive, I needed to be enthusiastic, I needed to be strong but fair, and I certainly shouldn't take no for an answer. All of those lessons would apply in all sorts of areas as I moved forward.

Of course I was still an engineer in the army, which meant I was still playing a supporting role, by definition. I'd have to keep fighting to get to a position of true leadership, which was an uphill battle against all kinds of forces that wanted me to stay where I was.

Winning that battle would take me a few more years.

4

Saying "No" to "No"

Sarah Cockerham was the recreation supervisor for the city of Killeen, Texas, when I first laid eyes on her in the spring of 1982. I have a passion for sports, and she was the woman they said I had to go see in order to register my softball team in the local league. People say love at first sight is a myth, but it sure isn't a myth to me. It was clear to me in that initial encounter that I could spend the rest of my life with this woman.

There was just one problem: She wouldn't go out with me!

It turned out that Sarah came from a military family. Her dad was a master sergeant when he left the army, and her mom was a sergeant E-5 in the Women's Army Corps. Sarah had grown up in Texas since she was six months old, but her four older brothers and one older sister had moved all over the world with the military. It was tough, and they always let her know what a tough life it was. And the one thing her dad told her throughout her entire life, and especially right before he died at age fifty, when Sarah was just twelve, was, "Whatever you do, don't date a GI!"

Getting over that obstacle was pretty difficult, but I was getting pretty good at not taking "no" for an answer. I figured the same lessons would apply in my personal life, but it would just take some persistence. Boy, did it ever. I spent $690 on flowers trying to get Sarah to go out with me! It was a nonstop effort of flowers and phone calls until finally she agreed to come to my house for a Fourth of July party. It wasn't even a real date. My roommate and a whole bunch of other people were there, but standing next to Sarah watching the fireworks that night, I remember thinking, "This feels right."

My efforts were worth every penny. Sarah finally relented, and we went out on some real dates. I fell in love with everything she is, and she made me feel love like I'd never known. That October, I took her down to South Padre Island. Everything seems right to me when I'm at the beach, so I decided that was the place. We were standing knee-deep in the ocean when I pulled a ring out of my swim trunks and asked her to marry me. She said yes.

We got married that December 4, and life changed for me in that instant. Sarah became my top priority. My career was going great. I was in command of my second company there at Fort Hood. But every decision I made from that point forward would require her counsel, and everything I did would take her and our marriage into consideration first.

That change in priorities would grow even deeper the following October, when our daughter, Susan, was born. From my perspective, nothing mattered more than my family at that point. Nothing. Sarah and Susan would always come first. Before me. Before my career. Before everything. I was beginning to set the priorities in my life that would provide a solid foundation for me to stand on once I became a leader.

Of course, I still had quite a ways to go.

After six years at Fort Hood, I found out the hard way that I had extended my welcome just as far as it could be extended. The army doesn't like its soldiers to stay in one place, and it was time for me to move on. I tried to preempt some placement I didn't want by calling the engineer branch and telling them how thrilled I would be to command another company. But the army wasn't having it. They wanted to put me into a new role. And the role they decided to put me in was that of an army recruiter in Dayton, Ohio.

I don't mean any disrespect to the powers that be, but that seemed like a really, really dumb decision for my career—and an even worse decision for my family. We were an army family. We were prepared to go wherever the army sent us. We just didn't want to go to Dayton.

My apologies to the great people of Dayton, Ohio, but the idea of moving my family to that Midwestern city so I could spend my time as a recruiter sounded like a death sentence to my twenty-something ears. I offered to move almost anywhere else. Heck, I was willing to go overseas if I had to in order to command another company or take on a more interesting, leadership-oriented role. But the army simply said, "No." It was time to move on.

I had established a pretty good track record by this point for not taking "no" for an answer in any part of my life. So I kept on asking, over and over. I basically begged the army for another option—any option—until they finally presented me with a choice: "Well," they said, "instead of being a recruiter, you could go study this thing called robotics at either Stanford, MIT (the Massachusetts Institute of Technology), or Carnegie Mellon."

What was that? I could hardly believe my ears. After listening to my repetitive pleas, the army finally told me they would be willing to put me back in school—to send me to get my graduate degree instead of sending me off to be a recruiter. They were very interested in pursuing new technologies at that time, and the fact that I was an engineer officer—a role I didn't want to be in, don't forget—put me in the perfect position to do that. Obstacles/opportunities. You gettin' this?

I put down the phone, picked up the dictionary, and looked up *robotics*. Like a lot of people who grew up in the 1970s, the only robots I'd ever really heard of were the science-fiction kind. But what "robotics" meant as a field of study was to pursue the use of machines to perform tasks traditionally performed by human beings—especially repetitive tasks or tasks that needed to be performed in areas that could be hazardous, of which there were plenty to be found in the army. It sounded intriguing.

41

The idea of going back to school and being a student again hadn't really occurred to me at that stage of life, but I thought it would be a whole lot better than becoming a recruiter in Dayton, Ohio. Sarah agreed! So I went ahead and applied to MIT.

I was accepted six weeks later. I moved my young family up to Boston, Massachusetts, which is one heck of a far cry from Texas both in terms of culture and weather. But my wife saw the opportunity that lay before me and fully supported the move.

The school seemed pretty excited to have military officers in their midst. First of all, they didn't have to worry about financial assistance. The army was paying our tuition. And second, they knew they could count on the fact that officers do a pretty good job at completing assigned tasks (which corporate America knows a little something about, too. That's why there are so many ex-military officers serving in mid- to top-tier management positions at corporations all over this country). MIT was happy to have me, and at first, I was happy to be there.

There was just one problem: I had no idea how tough MIT was going to be.

I was used to being a big man on campus at West Point, at the very top of the class academically, and I received all A's in high school. But I got to MIT and the highest grade I managed to eek out of a test was a 52. I was always the lowest in the class. The bottom. The pits. It wasn't that I wasn't working hard. I was! It was just that I was hanging out with all of these professional students, and I couldn't seem to hold a candle to their performance in that world.

Remember all of the kids in your high school who wore pocket protectors and sat in the front row? They went to MIT. Academics meant everything to these students. They didn't do anything else. Never went anywhere else. In fact, I was convinced they only came out at night. They were like moles! And, oh, by the way, most of them had no idea about life outside of the university. Here I was with a wife and a seven-month-old daughter, having made it through Beast Barracks and West Point and six years at Fort Hood, while most of these students had no life experience outside of school and dorm life. But every one of them crushed me in the classroom.

It was such an ego blast to me after working so very hard. In fact, the one time I got a 52 on a test, my advisor accused me of cheating. He didn't think I was capable of doing even *that* well. I hadn't cheated, of course. What I had done was gone to the library and reviewed all of the previous tests in that subject, written down all of the answers, and memorized as many as I could. I worked hard to find a solution to the problem of continuously failing tests. And even then it only resulted in a 52 out of 100.

To say I was discouraged was an understatement. Every time I'd get a test back, I'd take the posture of giving up.

"I quit," I'd say to myself. "I'm going to the ROTC department and calling the army. I just quit."

Of course, I'd usually walk by a pay phone on the way to the ROTC offices, and since Sarah had followed me up there, I felt the need to tell her I was gonna quit before I went ahead and actually did it.

Lo and behold, each and every time I called her to tell her I was quitting, she'd say, "No, you're not. You brought me all the way up to Boston, I'm freezing cold, and you're gonna finish!"

Tough love. Just when I needed it most.

Both times in my early life that I was tempted to give in to the obstacle, someone else came through and pushed me forward. First it was my dad, with his tough love at West Point. And then there was Sarah, reminding me of my commitment at MIT. My dad and Sarah, telling me, "You're not gonna quit." And I'm grateful to both of them.

Sometimes we need that extra push in life. Sometimes we need that helping hand. You need to be willing to listen to the people you trust, to accept the help that they're offering in your times of struggle, even if they're telling you something you don't necessarily want to hear.

Many years later I participated in the Bud Light series of triathlons—a combination one-mile open-water swim, twenty-six-mile bike race, and six-mile run. And in each of those grueling races, my training partner was the one person who kept me from quitting.

Believe me, no matter how passionate you are about sports—and I am—in the middle of that test of human endurance, you want to quit! In fact, I almost drowned during the Chicago triathlon. There were six-foot waves and the water was 60 degrees. It was miserable. But even in those conditions my training partner got me through. He pushed me to finish the race. It was a fitting metaphor for facing down obstacles in my life, for sure.

Whenever I've come up against an obstacle, it seems, somebody's been there to help me over the hurdle. I think God puts those people in your life for a reason. And as life has proceeded, I've helped plenty of people over their own hurdles in return. That's just the way it works. The results of those extra-effort, getting-over-the-hurdle moments in life are filled with opportunity. Almost by definition.

Just as West Point turned from Beast Barracks into the launching pad for my entire army career, enduring the low grades and repeated blows to my self-esteem in order to complete my master's degree in robotics at MIT would turn into an immeasurably large opportunity for me as well. Robotics was the wave of the future. My knowledge in the field would separate me from my peers in the army, and push me to the forefront—not only during my army career, but in my post-army career as well, as I moved on to consult for major robotics-centered technology firms. My knowledge and expertise in that field, which would be bolstered through years of further experience in the army itself, would also lead to my landing a job at the University of Texas at Arlington, where I was appointed to the position of executive director of the University at Arlington Research Institute just a few months after my retirement from the army in January of 2012.

When I trace back to the roots of my current position in life, it boils down to this: I listened to my wife. I didn't quit. And—oh yeah—I refused to sit back and take "no" for an answer when I knew that answer wasn't what I wanted or needed in my life and/or career.

5

Changing Career Paths

Soon after graduating from West Point, in year three of serving in the army, I started pushing to transfer to a different branch. It was clear as day to me that as an engineer officer, I would spend my entire career working for somebody else. That's not what I wanted. I wanted to be the guy in charge. The only way to do that, as far as I could see, was to branch-transfer. My first choice was to be an armor officer, but nobody wanted me to branch-transfer.

"No. You can't do that" was the answer from on high. "There's a shortage of engineer officers. We don't need you as an armor officer."

For nine years after West Point, I accepted "no" for an answer. But I never stopped asking for it. I never gave up trying.

People tend to want to keep you in a box. Whatever role you started out in, somehow, structured organizations of all shapes and sizes—from the army to colleges to big corporations—want to keep you there. If you're on a certain career path, there's this inherent pressure built into the system to keep you on that career path whether you like it or not. I've never understood where that comes from, and I've simply never stood for that behavior. In life, we need to choose our paths to follow our call, to go after whatever it is we want to go after, or we're never going to be fulfilled.

That belief was driven home for me even further prior to wrapping up my studies at MIT. In August of 1985, my wife gave birth to our beautiful son, Lucas. Just as my marriage had refocused my purpose in life, and just as the birth of my daughter, Susan, had refocused my priorities, the birth of Lucas sharpened my desire to do right by my family first, in everything I did. As you know, I didn't have much of anything growing up. I wanted to give my kids so much more than my parents gave me. Not the material things, so much, but the backbone and guidance they needed to succeed in life, whatever they chose to do.

After graduating with my master's degree from MIT, I was assigned to and stationed at Fort Knox, Kentucky. I remember driving down there from Boston in a little Toyota Corolla with my wife, our young daughter, a six-week-old son, and a mini dachshund named Squirt all stuffed into that compact car. We slept on the floor of our new home the first night because we didn't have any furniture!

It was there at Fort Knox where I was given a new title: Robotics Project Officer. I was still an engineer. I still worked for the engineer branch of the army. It was a forward-thinking position, on the cutting edge of new technologies in the field that would slowly change the way we do business on the battlefield—looking ahead to the unmanned vehicles and drones that are in operation all over the world as part of our armed forces today. But the title did little to put me on the leadership track I wanted to be on. And now, for my family as much as for me, I wanted to be on that track more than ever.

Lucky for me, I went to work for a major general named Tom Tait—a man who would become one of my mentors. Tom was a guy who recognized my strengths and abilities, and was willing to go the extra mile for me.

One day General Tait and I flew from Fort Knox over to Fort Monroe, Virginia, to brief another general on an armored cavalry program. I presented the standard overview that you might present

46

in a boardroom, to which the other general commented, "Hey, that's a great brief."

He then turned to General Tait and said, "Why do you have an engineer officer working this?"

General Tait said right then and there, "I can fix that."

On the flight home, Tait turned to me and said the words I'd almost given up hope of ever hearing: "You want to be an armor officer?"

"Sir, I've been trying to be an armor officer for *nine years*," I said.

We land. He picks up the phone. He calls the armor branch chief in Washington, D.C., and says, "If you don't get Lynch branch-transferred, you're fired."

A lot of wheels went into motion, and next thing I know the branch transfer's approved. Just like that, I'm an armor officer. For all those years I had kept the faith and continued to strive. I felt like I was finally getting my reward. It brought to mind Matthew 25:21: "His master replied, 'Well done, good and faithful servant! You have been faithful with a few things; I will put you in charge of many things. Come and share your master's happiness!'"

The thing is, everybody—and I mean everybody—told me not to make that transfer. Let me explain why everyone was so against it.

I was an established engineer officer. In general terms, the army promotes you according to years of service. But we have a system in place that dictates that if there's someone who's clearly a cut above, we can select him or her for promotion early. My entire career I was selected for promotion early. By the end of my career, I was one of the youngest three-star generals in the army because I worked hard, prayed hard, and got promoted early time and time again.

The fact that I was already nine years in as an engineer officer meant I was pretty far along on a well-established career path in that branch, so everybody assumed that if I branch-transferred, my career would be over. That's in-the-box thinking at its worst. The general consensus was that by jumping over to armor, I would be erasing my nine years of career progress and starting from scratch. "They're never going to let you command a tank battalion because you were never a tank platoon leader or a tank company commander," they said. "You just don't have the experience!" That was a risk I was willing to take.

Pushing outside the box was certainly going to present more obstacles, but I expected those obstacles to soon become opportunities. My first assignment as an armor officer was in the Eleventh Armored Cavalry Regiment. The regimental commander there, knowing I'd never been a tank platoon leader or tank company commander, decided to make me the regimental logistics officer. That's purely a support position, not operations. This felt like a huge step backward.

I got why the assignment was made. All of my peers in the armor branch had been tank platoon leaders and tank company commanders. They had spent ten years working their way up to the position. And here I was, this new guy putting on armor brass without any kind of professional background. I could have easily said right there, "Okay. I didn't branch-transfer so I could be the guy counting toilet paper. That's not what I came to do." I could've quit. But I had learned a thing or two about not quitting by that time in my life, and I didn't need an outside voice to tell me to stick with it. Just like it had been at MIT and West Point, I knew that this was only an obstacle. Nothing more. Rather than just give up, I said to myself, "Okay, I'm going to work my way through this."

I did the best I could. I followed my own rules: I worked hard, just like my mom taught me, and I didn't complain; I made myself widely known so the higher-ups knew me and could see what a good job I was doing. And it worked. Just three months later I was selected to become an operations officer for the First Squadron, Eleventh Armored Cavalry Regiment. Operations officer was just where I wanted to be as a field officer. Much like the chief operating officer at a corporation, the operations officer generally runs the unit. They plan activities, allocate resources, and maneuver forces on the battlefield. It is the job all aspiring commanders want in order to prepare them for command. It was perfect.

My wife made a pretty big move in her own career while we were stationed in Kentucky. She decided to go back to school, eventually earning her master's degree in education from the University of

Louisville. And she did this while juggling a home, two kids, a dog, and me! If that's not proof that you can get it all done and get what you want if you're willing to put in the hard work and dedication, I don't know what is. Sarah never fails to amaze and impress me.

We both made bold moves, and those moves paid off.

Because I was moved into the armor branch, I would be stationed in Germany when the Warsaw Pact crumbled and the wall came tumbling down. I was there in the Fulda Gap when the East Germans came into West Germany and experienced freedom for the first time. I witnessed that great moment in history firsthand because I had made the decision to branch-transfer from engineer to armor and accept that risk. I made that decision even though the army and everyone I knew threw all of those obstacles up and said, "You ought not do it!"

My branch-transfer decision was not only a success, it was also the jump-start I needed to set me on the path toward a successful career that would culminate in my becoming a general.

If I had given in to that pressure and not followed my heart, I never would have moved up to become a flag officer, I never would have been a division commander or corps commander. It was a life-changing experience. All because of this guy named Tom Tait, who had the audacity to pick up the phone and say, "You're branch-transferring Lynch or you're fired."

Could my career have come to a screeching halt after I made that transfer? Yes! In some ways, making that branch-transfer was the ultimate risk. But I knew that it was something I needed to do, and I was determined not to let that transfer stop the momentum of my career, no matter what. I simply wasn't comfortable being the support guy. I knew that. I wanted to be the guy in charge. I knew I didn't like to be the guy in the back of the room who hoped nobody would ask him a question. That wasn't me. I wanted to be the guy in the front of the room. The guy who asks the questions, and whom people would ask questions *of*.

Eventually I would get a chance to do that on a far bigger scale than I ever could have imagined.

6

The Digital Battlefield

The speed at which technology advances gets faster and faster each year. It's a daunting thing when you think about it. Our kids and grandkids today take for granted the kind of technological advances that were pure science fiction back when you or I were in high school and college! When Epcot Center opened at Disney World in Florida, in 1982, they had "futuristic" displays that incorporated "video phones" from some distant time when we might actually be able to see the person we're talking to on a big television-like screen in addition to hearing them. Today it seems like every six-year-old has been on Skype on their mommy's tablet or notebook, or FaceTimed their grandma on the iPhone in the palm of their hand—as naturally as if it's always been there. Heck, those cell phones themselves, those handheld wireless communication devices that we all carry around and curse about when the signal drops, the very thought of their existence was equated with spaceships and far-out planets on *Star Trek* as recently as the 1970s. We've already eclipsed that sci-fi handheld wireless communicator vision with smartphones, high-speed wireless Internet connections, and who knows what'll come next?

Technology flies. The best leaders not only embrace that fact, but jump right into the pilot's seat during the test-flight stage of any new technology that might benefit their organization and stay far ahead of the competition—even if that means taking some pretty big risks along the way.

Of course, when it comes to adopting technology or just about anything else that's "new," any leader or forward-thinking employee at any company in America can tell you this fact: The hardest thing about getting a new idea *in* is getting the old idea *out*.

Back in the mid-1990s, the army decided to create a digital brigade, the 1st Brigade, 4th Infantry Division. Because of my background at MIT, I had established myself as a leader who was comfortable using new technology. So the army decided to make me the commander of that brigade.

What the army realized was that we were struggling on the battlefield. We weren't even at war then, but we were using this area at the National Training Center in Barstow, California, to conduct military training and explore the complexities of a potential battle with the Soviet Union or anyone else in the modern era. This was 1997. And one of the problems we had on the battlefield, especially in a place like the Mojave Desert (which was a pretty good approximation of what we'd find on the sands of Iraq a decade later), is that it was pretty easy to get lost. We'd be out there fighting, and we didn't know where we were.

Now, I know there are plenty of old-school military guys who will puff up their chests and tell you they always had their bearings, but it just wasn't true. There were battlefields throughout history, let alone in those war-game scenarios, where we didn't know where we were, we didn't know where our buddies were, and we sure as heck had no stinking clue where the enemy was.

We'd have these formations: If you're a tank platoon leader, you've got four tanks; if you're a tank company commander, you've got ten tanks; if you're a battalion commander, you've got forty-five tanks, and in the heat of battle you'd lose track of who went where. So we decided to use digitization as an opportunity to promote "situational awareness," which we defined as knowing where you are, knowing where your buddies are, and knowing (at least approximately) where the enemy is.

That all started in the mid-1990s, and they tested this in one experimental brigade—the brigade that I commanded.

The biggest obstacle to this whole thing working was that nobody wanted to give up their maps. Nobody wanted to throw out the way it *used to* be in anticipation of how it *could* be. I wound up in a situation where there were more people watching me with clipboards in their hands taking notes about all the things that didn't work than there were people working for me. It was so brand-spanking-new, everyone was nervous and just looking for any reason to give up and stick to the way things had been. But there were those of us who knew what the future might hold, and we were just trying to figure it all out. We didn't know if it would work, or how it would work, but we knew the world was changing—and we wanted to be on the forefront of that change.

Technology's a tricky animal. I remember one time as a full colonel, I was doing a major training exercise with this brigade, and the corps commander, a three-star general, came walking in and said, "Rick, brief me on your situation." Right then, in that moment, everything stopped working. I call it Murphy's Law of Technology: It's not *if* the technology's going to fail, but *when* it's going to fail, and it *always* fails at the worst possible time. Since it was fairly early on in the development of this new tracking technology, I didn't have any backup system in place, which meant I stood there looking pretty silly to the corps commander. I learned the hard way that I needed an analog backup to the digital systems we were introducing, because those digital systems were occasionally going to break down.

Nowadays, when everybody's got GPS devices in their cars and on their smartphones, this seems like pretty simple stuff. But we put systems on all of our vehicles that allowed us to track them not only from a central location, but allowed those systems to talk to each other and talk to headquarters. I could look at a digital screen and see where everybody was; and everybody on the battlefield could determine where everybody else was, too. You can imagine how many lives that could save when it comes to the avoidance of friendly fire situations alone. We also had reporting mechanisms in place so we could report where the enemy was, and then we used algorithms to extract where the enemy was going to be at any given time.

Back in 1997, this was a big deal. Most homes that had Internet service were still using dial-up connections, and Internet providers were trying to sell customers on higher bandwidth. It could easily take fifteen minutes to load a single high-quality digital photo onto the screen on your desktop. And here we were playing real-time digital warfare in the desert in California. It was awesome!

Fast-forward six or seven years beyond this trial-and-error stuff, and we actually had situational dominance in Iraq—situational dominance being "situational awareness" combined with "situational understanding." It allowed us to win, to reduce casualties, and more.

The digital brigade was a clear example of an opportunity, not an obstacle. But not everyone felt that way, and thankfully those of us who did feel that way prevailed. If we'd have looked at the early tests and just said, "This is too hard. These systems aren't working and it ain't worth the effort," then we wouldn't be as dominant on the battlefield as we are today. The art of applying advanced technology to improve your capability is not always easy and not always clear, especially since it always continues to evolve. But it's a necessary part of adaptation in the modern world, and continues to be of paramount importance in the army even now, after I've retired. Unmanned systems are the next wave—robotics that will be used to take human soldiers out of dirty, dull, or dangerous tasks, and will help save hundreds if not thousands of individual lives. I'm working on all sorts of projects with that end-goal in mind as we speak. And all of it traces back to those early challenging days in the mid-1990s.

The digitization of our armed forces was an act of courage. We were boldly going where no man had gone before. Taking the risk of trying these new systems and knowing that, potentially, they weren't going to work was important. Having the audacity to try this new capability, but at the same time having enough common sense to retain some analog capability as well, truly mattered. There were forces at play that wanted to put an end to it, that insisted it was a waste of time and money. We certainly know better today.

It's the same sort of forces that leaders in corporate America come up against all the time. The thing is, it's up to leaders to know when it's worth it to take the risk. You have to trust your gut and your experience, and be willing to take calculated risks in the name of progress, of advancement, of adaptation to the rapidly changing world around you. You have to be willing to try something that may or may not work as part of a long-term look at progress for your organization.

Using all of the army's new digital systems down in Barstow toward the end of my two years, I commanded a brigade of five thousand soldiers in a mock battle against a force using traditional measures—guys with maps, basically—and I'll admit to you here and now that we got our butts kicked. The digital brigade lost, and lost big. It was a laser-tag battlefield. Nobody was dying, but it was quite a blow. We accepted the fact that some of our systems worked and some didn't. But I never stopped looking at that last statement with an optimist's eye: "Some of the systems worked." So it wasn't a loss. Not to me, and not to any other champion of the digitization of the army. It was the early stages of trial and error. The research and development phase, if you will. And those early tests allowed us to move forward to finally get to the point we're at today.

Where are we today? Talk to any soldier and he or she will tell you: The difference between winning and losing on today's battlefield is situational awareness. When I led the surge in Iraq in 2007, my battle space was the size of the state of West Virginia. Thanks to the technology I helped launch a decade earlier, I knew where my people were at all times. Not just a few people, but 25,000 soldiers. That's 25,000 American heroes with their lives on the line. I knew where our equipment was, too. Billions of dollars' worth of equipment. I could toggle down on a single vehicle anywhere in that battle space and tell you who was in that vehicle at any moment. If we hadn't done the work of experimentation in the late 1990s, this situational awareness would have been an impossibility.

It took us a decade to work through all the bugs of what we were doing. Thankfully people had the foresight and fortitude to work through it—and to push back against the forces that would have kept us from moving forward. Lives were saved because of it. Lots of lives. On both sides.

Adapting to change, including technological change, is a major key to survival.

I'm happy that I was one of the people who pushed us forward, not one of the people who tried to stop progress from happening on the battlefield. I'm glad to have stuck around to see those changes in action, and to witness the rewards of our willingness to try, fail, learn, try again, and improve until we got it right.

Ten years from now, will you be able to say the same in your own field?

7

Learning From Poor Leadership

I was just a young captain the first time I found myself working for a completely useless leader. Everything this particular colonel did aggravated me. He was one of these guys with an ego as big as the room, and everything he did was about himself. His attitude was, "I'm *going* to be a general and you all are going to *make* me a general!" No matter what I spoke to him about, he just wouldn't listen. He didn't care.

Working for a boss who's incompetent, a horrible person, an unqualified dolt, or worse is one of the most frustrating things any forward-thinking employee, volunteer, soldier, or want-to-be leader ever faces. Answering to someone who's maybe not as smart as you are, or who looks down on their workers, or who is only in the job to fulfill some ego trip or personal agenda that has nothing to do with the task at hand—boy, I can feel my blood pressure rising just thinking about it! Can't you? We've all been there. We've all had to deal with a bad boss or a lousy teacher or a hypocritical leader at one point or another. It's just a part of life.

The thing is, what you choose to do with that experience is up to you.

In the case of this colonel, it came to a head one day when I went home to Sarah saying, "I'm either going to hit this guy or quit!" The hotheaded young man in me thought it was just not worth the pain to put up with this guy, and since I knew how much trouble I'd be in if I hit him, I honestly started thinking that the only way out of the situation might be to resign from the army.

Well, Sarah managed to calm me down to the point where I didn't do either. "No, you're not going to hit him," she said, and, "No, you're not going to quit. You're going to continue to persevere." (Have I mentioned what a blessing it's been to have Sarah in my life? She's been my saving grace more times than I can count. Having that one person who always has your best interest at heart, and who knows how to set you straight, is important in life.)

So I went back to work. But the whole time I was under this guy felt like wasted time. I was fuming. I felt like my whole career was at a standstill. I couldn't wait until it was over.

Boy, oh boy. As I look back on it now, I realize that I missed an extraordinary opportunity. I was so caught up in feeling angry and feeling sorry for myself for having to work under this lousy leader, I missed an opportunity that was staring me in the face.

I wouldn't miss it the next time.

A few years later I wound up serving under a leader who was the absolute antithesis of anything good in life.

This was one of those guys who loved to talk the talk, as if he were some moral superior we should all get down and worship. He had this three-by-five card on which he'd written his "philosophy," and he made every soldier carry a copy of that philosophy themselves, proclaiming the values by which we should all operate to make this battalion successful. The thing was, he didn't follow anything on the card! Everything he did was 180 degrees from the values on that card.

There is no quicker way to lose the trust of your subordinates than to say one thing and do another. This guy proved it every day.

Let me give you one example. One of the things this leader held in his "philosophy" was pretty basic: We should all support each other in the battalion; we should all have each other's back.

I think it's pretty obvious that having each other's back, in any work environment, involves a little bit of getting to know your co-workers. That fact just happens to be amplified in the army.

The army is a social environment. When you and your family are moved around to different locations, whether overseas or at any of the bases here in the United States, you have to learn to make friends quickly. Getting together at one another's houses for some food and a few beers is just a normal course of business. Well, this particular leader decided that we as an organization would not have a social life. His wife didn't like social activity, so he decided none of us should have social activities. As a result, no one in the battalion got to know each other very well, and basically we were all just miserable. Not just us soldiers, but our wives and kids, too.

We were about four months into this and it was clear that there was a need for some of us to get together, so Sarah and I hosted a little gathering at our house. It wasn't subversive. The army is a social environment, and this was part of filling a need. We did this on a Saturday night, on our own private time, and we didn't make a big deal out of it. We had a wonderful time. Everybody had a blast. It was really uplifting for the whole group.

Wouldn't you know it? At 6:30 Monday morning I get a call to report to his office. He locks my heels in front of his desk and starts screaming at me: "You're the most disloyal son of a gun I've ever met! Who do you think you are, having a party at your house? Who do you think you are, trying to advocate having *fun*?"

I somehow kept from yelling back, but even the way he handled that situation was an example of how, in my opinion, he was the absolute antithesis of a good leader. I didn't mind that he disagreed with my behavior; what I minded was the way he handled it. Not to mention the fact that he was being a complete hypocrite.

That's when I decided to make a very positive change in my life.

From fairly early on in my career, I had kept notebooks on leadership. I observed the things my leaders said and did, and kept notes on them. I figured, *If this guy's doing something that works, and he's in a position of leadership that I'd like to be in someday, the least*

I should do is make note of it and then do my best to emulate that behavior when I become a leader myself! It seemed pretty logical. It made sense to me to try to learn to copy the behavior of leaders I admired.

Dealing with this lousy leader made me see something else that was worth taking notes on: behaviors that as a leader, I would never, ever want to exhibit myself.

So I started a notebook titled "Thoughts on Battalion Command." My greatest aspiration in the army was to become a battalion commander, so I used the negatives of this terrible leader's words and actions as a guideline. The way I would become a successful battalion commander was to do the opposite of everything this guy did. Someday I would take what he did, all of those things that I wrote down in this notebook, and do exactly the opposite.

Fighting him at the time would have had no upside. He was my leader. I had to answer to him, like it or not. If I'd have been disrespectful or hurtful, or if I'd have called him names, I would have been relieved of my position. So I didn't do that. I tried to soldier on, to just get through it. And I did.

As a result, I learned a lot, and I told myself, "If I ever get to that level, I'm not going to be like that." Well, guess what? I did get to that level, and far beyond. And I think of that lousy leader all the time—as a simple self-check to make sure I do absolutely nothing that he ever did.

I've since advocated that approach to all of my subordinates. "Keep these notebooks. Watch what you're seeing. If you like it and it works for you, write it down, and when you get to that position, do it. If it doesn't work and you don't like it? Don't do it."

Having the ability to pay attention to what you're seeing and experiencing, and to listen and learn from what's right in front of you, is one way to take almost any obstacle—in this case a horrible boss or a terrible leader—and turn it into an opportunity. Even if it means paying attention to what's wrong, and learning exactly what not to do because of it.

8

Obstacles of Olympic Proportions

After serving in Germany through the fall of the Berlin Wall, my career in the army continued on a decidedly international track. I served in the first Gulf War on the ground in Kuwait. I'll talk more about my experience there later on. After a few years home, I went on to serve as the operations manager for Joint Forces Command, Naples, Italy, a NATO command overseeing missions in Bosnia, Kosovo, and Macedonia—all of which would eventually lead to my career as a general officer in a post-9/11 world, and my multiple roles in the war in Iraq.

Let me tell you, for a kid from a paper-factory town in Ohio to wake up in the middle of a country like Kosovo is a shock on many levels. The language and cultural barriers you face in many of these foreign countries is enough to make even the smartest among us feel ridiculously under-educated. There's almost no amount of studying or preparation you can do that will ever make you feel like a native. There are so many cultural subtleties to try and grasp, and in the heat of war, or even in the aftermath of war, those cultural subtleties can sneak up on you when you least expect it.

The reason the army sent me off to Kosovo was not only because they thought I was the right man for the job, but because they wanted me to get experience in understanding peace support operations and multinational operations. Kosovo Force (KFOR), a multinational force of about 12,000 people that NATO created in order to keep the peace, was being commanded by a French lieutenant general when I arrived. His deputy was a German major general. I started out as deputy chief of staff for operations, and later I became the chief of staff—overseeing a staff of six hundred from twenty-six nations. And I was the only American general on that staff!

I was pretty good at communicating by this point in my career. Or so I thought. I had daily meetings with my eight general officers on that staff. Two weeks into it, the French general came to me privately and said, "We all are required to speak English here, but we have *no idea* what you're saying!" It never occurred to me that my Texas colloquialisms didn't translate. When you're fixin' to talk to a multinational force, you can't use phrases like "fixin' to!"

It was a simple but important lesson: When you're working internationally, you have to learn to be precise in your communication. You can't risk having anyone in the room not understand what you're trying to say.

After working with NATO, I learned to keep my eyes open for cultural differences so I could prepare myself for conversations with enemies and allies alike. Attempts at keeping the peace required an understanding of cultural barriers and how to circumvent them. In fact, some of the cultural lessons I learned in Kosovo would come to serve me well in Iraq nearly a decade later.

One of the biggest realities I had to adapt to in multinational affairs overseas was accepting the fact that things just aren't always going to go our way, sometimes for very deep-seated, cultural, and political reasons. As Americans, we like to jump in, call the shots, and expect that everything's going to work out. Two problems we have as a country right now is that we have a short-term memory, and we want to rush to a conclusion. President Clinton got us into Bosnia thinking we'd be there for one year—and we're still there to this day! Heck, we're still a presence in Germany; we've been there since World War II!

We always seem a bit surprised and dismayed when things don't work out exactly the way we expect them to. But we shouldn't get discouraged. Instead, we as leaders need to step back and assess the situation from every angle. My work in Kosovo in a post-war peace-keeping capacity with NATO provides a stark example of what I'm talking about. In the simplest of terms, we were trying to get the Kosovar Albanians to work friendly with the Kosovar Serbians. The fighting in this latest conflict was over. They needed to rebuild. They *needed* to work together. Why couldn't we go in there, help keep the peace for a while, and get out? Well, think of it this way: The Kosovar Albanians had been persecuted by the Serbians for the past century. An entire century. They wanted freedom from that persecution, and they wanted Kosovo to be a separate country from Serbia rather than a province of Serbia. They wanted freedom—something we take for granted in America. Regardless of whether the current conflict was over, the ongoing conflict and fight for freedom versus control wasn't going away. That caused tension, which caused continual violence. Serbs attacked Albanians, Albanians attacked Serbs. It was all we could do to watch out for hot spots and keep the peace as best we could while the political resolutions unfolded.

Many of us were frustrated by the violence. We could understand the historical significance of what was going on, but hadn't it gone on long enough? Wasn't it just time for these two sides to work out a resolution and be done with it?

One day, one of the leaders of the Kosovar Albanians came to me with a simple but much needed lesson in perspective: "General, you don't understand. The Serbs killed three of my brothers and ten of my cousins, and if you think I'm going to forgive them anytime soon, you're mistaken."

Just like that, all the politics and posturing went right out the window. I realized there were troubles here that were immediate and deeply personal. Yes, the political strife was deeply rooted. It stretched back decades, the way conflicts in the Middle East stretch back decades and even centuries. It's hard for us to understand this kind of ethnic identification. It's foreign to us. But we're not talking only about "sides" here. We're talking about families. We're talking about loved ones. We're talking about brothers, sisters, mothers, cousins, spouses, children. Leaders can't lose sight of the fact that it's the people who matter. The fighting over land and power and control and politics isn't about any of those things. It's about people. And it's the same in the business world, politics, and elsewhere.

The world is much smaller today than it used to be. It's true! Anyone in corporate America knows it. Competition is global, as are the obstacles and opportunities that business leaders never had to think about tackling before the Internet came into its own. The smaller the world gets, the more complicated it becomes, and business leaders have to be ready to adapt in the global environment at a moment's notice—while understanding that it might take a very long time to make inroads or find resolutions when you're working in other parts of the world. But we can't lose sight of the fact that the root of every organization, every province, every country, is its people.

No matter what part of the world you're in, asking the right questions, listening to what you're being told, and seeing the cultural differences as clearly as you can make all the difference. For me, that early lesson of Kosovo ethnic identification would stick with me and come to serve me well in Iraq. My ability to identify with the deep-seated differences in the Shia and Sunni populations, and to see the Iraqi people as just that—people—would allow me to make the most of my position in a very dangerous and difficult situation.

Saying "Yes!"

One of the biggest lessons I learned in my time spent overseas was that sometimes it pays to be the guy who says yes.

Sometimes leaders need to be willing take on tasks nobody else wants, and even to attempt to do what others might think is just about impossible. Isaiah 6:8 states: "Then I heard the voice of the Lord saying, 'Whom shall I send? And who will go for us?' And I said, 'Here am I. Send me!'"

That's certainly what I did in the summer of 2004.

Less than three years after the 9/11 attacks, the Summer Olympics were set to start in Athens, Greece, that August. As you can imagine, the fear of terrorist attacks happening during the games was extraordinarily high. And rightly so. The games were happening in a part of the world that was close in proximity to known terrorist cells operating in Afghanistan, Pakistan, and Iraq. Millions of people and any number of heads of state would be in attendance. And in what could only be seen as a bonus to the deviant minds inside al-Qaeda, the eyes of the world would be watching.

The pressure to keep the games safe grew so intense that the Greek government—at the very last minute—decided to ask NATO for help.

Somewhere along the line, someone decided that the best team to handle anti-terrorist security operations as a backup to the Greek's own forces would be the NATO Response Force. The Response Force was historically a toothless tiger: soldiers who did drills and stayed prepared but never saw any action because the NATO nations could rarely agree unanimously on putting them into service. The force comprised a total of 16,000 people from across the NATO nations, including special forces, ground troops, ships at our disposal in the Athens vicinity, air forces that could be called in if needed, and a sixty-person leadership staff that would serve from inside the Greek Pentagon. Nobody else wanted to take command of this outfit. A number of three- and four-star generals were asked to take on this mission before me, and all of them found some reason not to do it.

In some ways I don't blame them: It was clear that if something went wrong at the Olympics, this NATO Response Force would be to blame for it. And whoever was heading up the Response Force would receive the ultimate blame.

By the time this responsibility was presented to me, there were just three weeks before the torch was lit and the XVIII Summer Games began. Three weeks!

Confronted with the mission to deploy the DJTF (Deployable Joint Task Force) of the NATO Response Force to Athens for the Olympics on such short notice, I could easily have said, "This is too hard, go get somebody else." But I didn't. I looked at it as an opportunity to finally train this staff in a real-world mission, and a chance for me to lead a multinational force into action. So I said yes.

We were finally going to give this toothless tiger some teeth.

I threw everything I had into prepping the Response Force to be a terrorist watchdog group on the ground. We learned the ins and outs of the venue maps, knew where we wanted people positioned, prepped all kinds of possible scenarios and responses, and hit the ground running in Athens with confidence that we could pull this off—keeping athletes, dignitaries, politicians, and the public safe from harm. Our team was fired up because they were finally getting to do what they'd trained to do. There were a few glitches along the way, though. At one point I realized that about half of my staff was simultaneously attending and "keeping an eye on" a certain Summer Olympics event: women's beach volleyball. Heck, we had so many eyes on those bikini-clad bodies in the beach volleyball stadium, a terrorist couldn't have moved one inch without getting taken out! Much to my men's dismay, I had to order a whole bunch of them to move on to other venues, making sure all of the Olympics venues were being watched just as keenly. When all was said and done, the Response Force did its duty. The games were safe. The only thing history will remember about those games is who won gold. Had we not been there, tragedy might have struck.

When the mission was over, I think it's fair to say that the NATO Response Force as an organization was more coherent than it had been in its entire history. The entire Response Force was proud of what they did: "Look what we can accomplish!" was the new mantra. They had real-world experience to back them up.

Putting that Response Force to work on the ground was a blessing. We got more accomplished for the Response Force as an organization than any amount of planning, training, meetings, and "talking" ever could. Military people want to move to the sound of the guns. Putting aside family separations and the wariness one feels over the possibility of memorial services, there's not a soldier, sailor, air-man, or marine serving today who, if given a choice between being stateside or being in Iraq or Afghanistan, wouldn't want to be over there. Because that's what we're trained to do.

I think there's a lesson in that for the corporate world: Move to the sound of the guns. There's merit in the act of doing—of real-world experience versus planning, going to meetings, talking about stuff all the time, and then talking about it some more. Staleness sets in that way. "Let's have a meeting to plan the next meeting!" Leaders need to put a stop to it. Get your work force into spring-into-action mode. Go get stuff done. Stop talking about it and do it. Take a risk. Even if it goes wrong, at least it's going somewhere. And you'll all learn from the experience. Take a lesson from those Nike ads and "Just Do It." We'll all be better for it.

Looking back on those Olympics now, I realize that rushing to get my staff ready to roll that quickly taught me a few great lessons on efficiency, time management, and preparedness that would serve me well three years later, when I found myself with only six weeks to prepare a unit of 25,000 men for the surge in Iraq—one of the largest military undertakings our country would attempt in recent memory.

I gained the experience I needed by saying yes and taking a risk.

9

Facing the Media

On the heels of my success in Athens, the army sent me off to Iraq to serve as the deputy chief of staff for political, military, and economic affairs for the Multinational Force-Iraq (MNF-I). I said good-bye to my family once again and went to work in the United States Embassy in Baghdad. For two months in the spring of 2005 I adjusted to this new environment at the epicenter of the still-new war, and adjusted to my role as best I could. I attended Ambassador Zalmay Khalilzad's country team meetings. I would be deeply involved in attempting to build "capacity" in the Iraqi government and populations, which meant developing jobs, schools, industry, etc.

Iraq was in a state of despair. The people of Iraq, just like us, want freedom from fear. They want to have a job, they want to be able to provide for their families, they want to be able to send their kids to school, they want health care, and at that point in time they had none of that. It was a big job, a massive coalition team effort, and I felt like I was just starting to get a handle on things when General George Casey called me into his office.

"Rick, I know you came here to be the deputy chief of staff for political, military, and economic affairs, but in addition you're also now the spokesman for the force."

I was shocked. The spokesman for the force was the guy who stood in front of the television cameras and briefed the press on everything we were doing in Iraq. He was the guy you'd see on the evening news, the guy who had to answer everyone's questions. *Why on earth would General Casey want me for that role?*

I expressed my doubts and reservations to him as strongly as I could. I explained to him that I didn't have any particular training to do that, and didn't particularly *want* to do that—and he promptly reminded me that he was the man in charge. I had no choice.

The obstacle here was obvious: I had no training. I had never been a spokesperson before. Ever. The war in Iraq was one of the biggest military endeavors the United States had taken on in decades, and one that lately had been going south on us, which meant that being the spokesperson was akin to being on the firing line. I mean, there are people who like to deal with the media, but I had no particular affinity for doing that even under the best of circumstances. And to be frank, I didn't really know what I was doing. I could not understand why Casey had selected me for this.

Let me paint the picture for you: The year was 2005. It was a challenging time in the Iraq War. Casualty rates were high and costs were exorbitant, but we were making progress. Our basic bumper-sticker mission statement, which was put into place by Condoleezza Rice, was "Clear, hold, and build." Our army could do that. We could clear an area of those who were fighting back, we could hold an area and essentially stop the violence, and then we could get about rebuilding the infrastructure and facilities to help get the Iraqis back on their feet. The only problem was, once we did any of that, we'd have to move on to the next area—and often we didn't have enough troops to leave a security force in place once we left. From my perspective and the perspective of just about anyone who was over there at that time, we didn't have enough troops on the ground.

Our enemies would come to see that as an opportunity they could exploit.

The insurgents were continually attempting to drive a wedge between the Sunni and Shia populations already, causing constant tensions. But in February of 2006, they took it so far as to blow up the Golden Mosque in Samara, the most sacred Shia shrine in Iraq. They started kidnapping and killing local businessmen and politicians. They did everything they could to keep the Iraqi people in a state of despair so they would be more pliable when it came to hating the Americans.

It got to a point where we would build a school or a bridge, and the very next day the insurgents would come and blow it up. They would target Iraqis who appeared to have helped us in our efforts, and either kill them or kill their families, destroying everything they loved. That drove a massive wedge into our ability to elicit cooperation from the people we needed most: the Iraqi population whom we were trying to help.

That whole situation was just beginning to develop when General Casey made me spokesman.

It took an awful lot of prayer for me to find a way to go into this with a positive attitude, and even more prayer to find the "opportunity" in this tremendous obstacle that lay before me.

But I did it. Despite the obstacles at hand, I realized that an opportunity had presented itself: the opportunity to improve my communication skills. People had always told me that strategic communication and knowing how to deal with the media were important. The army gave us all kinds of instructional talks about dealing with the media, and yet I hadn't been paying particular attention to it. I was hoping—nay, assuming—I'd never have to be the guy talking to the press!

After that conversation with General Casey, I could have thrown up my hands, said I'm not prepared, and possibly found some way out of it. After all, who wants to learn their lessons on dealing with the media *in front of the media*? But instead I prayed, I put my head down, I got to work and found an even bigger opportunity in that obstacle—an opportunity to help tell the story of the very real progress we were making in Iraq. Having been the political-military-economic guy for those two months, it was clear to me that even with the lack of sufficient troops, and even with the destruction caused by the insurgents, we were making some progress. Progress on the governmental side, the economic side, and also in building clinics and providing other various needs of the Iraqi people. It floored me that no one back home seemed to know about any of that. That very important story wasn't being told.

I can help communicate to the American people the progress we're making in Iraq, I thought. If that's not an opportunity, I don't know what is.

Of course, I wouldn't be talking to *just* the American people. And that presented another challenge: How I could effectively communicate our message, knowing that we were basically talking to three separate groups every time we went on television or talked to the papers? Every time I spoke I would be talking not only to the American people, but also to the Iraqi people *and* to the insurgents. They would all be watching!

As spokesperson, my primary venue was live press conferences. Every Thursday I'd have to stand in front of this gaggle of reporters, all of whom were looking for bad news and looking to put the general on the spot. I would go back to headquarters and see myself on television—FOX, CNN, everywhere. What was said at this press conference was always considered newsworthy, because everyone was trying to figure out what was going on in Iraq at that time. So everything I said was transmitted instantly back to the States.

Talk about pressure. One misstep and I'd be skewered!

I wound up on Jon Stewart's *The Daily Show* one time—and not in a good way. I was doing a press conference talking about Abu Musab al-Zarqawi, the infamous Jordanian terrorist. We had captured some video of Zarqawi basically acting stupid. He was wearing white tennis shoes, and he burned his hand on the barrel of a hot machine gun. He was clearly a nut job. So as part of our communication, I was trying to show the world—including the insurgents and the Iraqi people—"Look at this guy; he's an idiot!"

Jon Stewart wound up playing my entire piece that night, including my statement in front of the microphones: "Watching Zarqawi," I said, "is one of those things that makes you go 'Hmm.'" At which point Stewart stopped the clip and said directly to the camera, "It makes you go, 'Hmm . . . How come we haven't caught him?!'"

It's hard not to feel dumb when you've put your own foot in your mouth like that. It was a miscalculation on my part. In thinking about how those tapes would play to the insurgents and the Iraqis, I forgot to think through how it might make us look back in the States. But like all mistakes, it was (once again) something to learn from.

The entire experience was an opportunity to develop a new skill set that has served me very well. If I had not taken on that spokesperson role, I would not have been nearly as successful in my future roles as a division commander, corps commander, or IMCOM commander.

I've thanked George Casey numerous times in the years since for giving me that opportunity. I didn't thank him at the time, that's for sure! But his belief in me helped me develop a whole new skill set. And that spokesperson role gave me a good feeling as I helped try to turn the news around.

Of course, trying to turn the news around is a skill set all its own. Just as I thought it might, stepping into that role taught me firsthand about the art of strategic communication. What is strategic communication? "Consistent themes and messages delivered at high frequency over multiple media." And it's something every leader ought to be aware of and advocating for within his or her organization whenever necessary.

At one point I had a senior editor of one of the most influential newspapers in the United States in my office in Baghdad, and I said to him, "I'm taking all of your reporters out to see good things and bad things. Why is it that the only thing that ever shows up in your newspaper is the bad things?" And he said to me, "Bad news sells newspapers."

I'd take the television affiliates out—NBC, ABC, CBS, FOX, BBC—with their camera crews, and I'd show them schools being built, clinics being built, kids in school, governmental process in action. They'd get good footage of all of that, and then all I'd ever see on television is footage of the most recent explosion.

"If it bleeds, it leads." That saying is terrible and true.

How could I get the real story out when the national media was so jaded and broken and clearly uninterested in writing about or airing anything that didn't "sell"?

It took me a little while, but what I finally realized is that the way to get the story out to the American people was not through the national media but through the local media. The local media was looking for "good news" stories of their men and women making a difference. So I had a great opportunity there, not only to do interviews myself, but also to empower our soldiers and others with information so that when they went home they could go right to the local media and tell their stories of progress.

That same approach can work for corporations and other organizations. The opportunity is still there to get "good" stories out via the local media. It's not easy. You can't blanket the airwaves all at once with a single media hit. And yet the effectiveness of spreading the word on the ground through local media, one town, city, county, or state at a time, can make a significant difference in whatever message it is you're trying to send.

It's exhausting work, I've gotta say. I certainly wished there was one show, one newspaper I could have gone to. But even when I had big media coverage from Katie Couric or some other media giant, getting the word out on the good we'd done was a very tough road. That's all there is to it. It's tough!

Just to give you a sense of how tough it can be to get your message out, I'll share with you an impromptu moment that happened after I came home from Iraq and took over command at Fort Hood. This particular moment came many months after I had that run-in with the army wife on the street—the run-in that prompted me to order all soldiers home for dinner with their families at 6:00 p.m. sharp. I had been featured in papers big and small, and all over local television and radio. Everyone was proclaiming me the "family-first general." We had become the family-first corps with all of the programs I'd put into place to help families reconnect and make the most of their time together on base.

74

News of my progress spread far and wide, and one time when General Casey and his wife, Sheila, came into town, they said, "Hey, since you're the family-first general, we'd really like to meet some of the families and see how it's going."

Now, I never stage these sorts of conversations. I never pick people in advance and say, "When asked this question, give this answer." I'd rather hear the truth, no matter how harsh it might be. So there was this group of families and soldiers sitting in this conference room, and Sarah and I were sitting in the back of the room, and George asked the question: "What do you think of the family programs here at Fort Hood?" A young private's wife stood up and said, "There aren't any family programs here."

I felt like I was gonna sink right through my chair. I had spent eighteen months building those programs, and yet in this one instance, this particular young woman didn't know about any of them. This just proves the point that you can have the best programs in the world, but if nobody knows about them, you might as well not even have them. Getting the word out is important stuff. Having some media savvy, I believe, is crucial for any leader.

As I moved on to other roles in my career, I always made it my business to learn everything I could about how people were getting their information, and then worked to get my message out to those outlets.

The thing some people forget is that both of those elements have to work together, in tandem, or the message simply won't be heard. I remember when I was working at the Pentagon, I went out to visit one of our army installations, and the garrison commander was so proud to show off this public service announcement he put together on energy conservation, which had started airing on the local on-post television station. Later that day he took me to speak to five hundred family members, and during my presentation I asked the group, "How many of you watch the local on-post television station?" Only two people raised their hand! I didn't mean to embarrass the guy. I was just curious. Turns out, his message that he was so proud of wasn't being heard by anyone that he hoped would hear it. And that's a failure by any measure.

I ask that question all the time now: "Where do you get your information? Is it television, radio, the newspaper, or the Internet?" And the answer these days, from 90 percent of the people I talk to, is the Internet, usually through social media like Facebook, Twitter, etc. When you get into this a little bit, you quickly realize that if you're going to communicate to people, you've got to communicate to them in a medium that they actually consume. Otherwise you're just wasting your time.

As I talk to corporate America, that's an important point: "How are your potential customers or clients accessing their information?" It's not all the same.

Knowing enough to ask that question and seek out the answers will present new opportunities for you to get your message out. And then it's up to you to take advantage of that opportunity.

Actually, I suppose that's the real key to all of these obstacle/opportunity lessons, isn't it? Becoming a leader takes a whole lot more than just getting over the obstacles and getting the job done. It takes seeing the opportunities in the obstacles, and taking advantage of those opportunities whenever you can. That's a big difference. And the difference will affect how far you get on the road to success—both your own success as well as the success of those around you and beneath you in whatever leadership role you take on.

PART 2

LIFESTYLE EVANGELISM

Let your light shine before others, that they may see your good deeds and glorify your Father in heaven.

Matthew 5:16

Leaders lead by example.

They don't just talk the talk; they walk the walk. In every aspect of life.

I have always tried to lead the way I would want to be led, and I hope you see examples of that throughout this book. I don't always succeed. I'm not perfect, and I don't even pretend to be. But I do my best to show my leadership style through my actions. To show strength by being strong; to show perseverance by persevering; to demonstrate work-life balance by balancing my work life and my family life, and so on.

"Lifestyle evangelism," the way I define it, has nothing to do with any particular religion. Yes, I am a man of faith, and my faith is the cornerstone of my strength as a leader. When it comes to prioritizing my life, God comes first, family second, and career third. How you prioritize your own life is, of course, up to you. But no matter how you prioritize your life, if you're going to be a leader, it's important that you become a lifestyle evangelist: that your actions match your words, and that the example you set in the way you lead and live your life helps to inform and inspire those you're leading.

When it comes to commanding troops—be they your work force, your team, your community, your students, or your soldiers on a desert battlefield—leading by example is far more effective than all the preaching in the world. We can talk all we want. But it's the examples we set through our own deeds and actions that command respect and truly make a difference.

10

Finding Faith

My journey to God was a rather long one, by most standards. My parents never took me to church. Ever. We were a Christian household, and my mother and father were both believers. They just didn't believe in the tenets of organized religion, so the only time I ever stepped foot inside a church in my youth was when one of the neighbors asked my brother and me if we'd like to come along.

In fact, my most vivid "religious experience" back in Ohio was when I was maybe nine or ten years old. A Baptist minister knocked on our front door and wound up coming inside, where he sat in our living room and told my parents that they were going to hell because they smoked and drank.

"And your children are going to hell, too, because they aren't baptized!"

That was all my dad could take before he stood up, grabbed that minister, and physically threw him out the front door.

It's important to understand that I didn't grow up with a particularly strong belief system. I wasn't indoctrinated into a particular church from a young age. I found God and the beliefs that now serve as the foundation of everything I stand for a bit later in life as an adult and of my own free will.

My first experience attending church on any regular basis was at West Point. I was a member of the very first class of cadets who weren't required to go to chapel on Sundays. But we all went anyway. It was just sort of implied that you had to go, like it or not. So I went. And while I listened and learned on those Sunday mornings—absorbing a few lessons along the way—the real lessons I learned on morals and values at West Point were summed up in the Cadet Prayer that we all had to memorize, and the Honor Code we were bound to live by.

The Cadet Prayer is this:

O God, our Father, Thou Searcher of human hearts, help us to draw near to Thee in sincerity and truth. May our religion be filled with gladness and may our worship of Thee be natural.

Strengthen and increase our admiration for honest dealing and clean thinking, and suffer not our hatred of hypocrisy and pretense ever to diminish. Encourage us in our endeavor to live above the common level of life. Make us to choose the harder right instead of the easier wrong, and never to be content with a half-truth when the whole can be won. Endow us with courage that is born of loyalty to all that is noble and worthy, that scorns to compromise with vice and injustice and knows no fear when truth and right are in jeopardy. Guard us against flippancy and irreverence in the sacred things of life. Grant us new ties of friendship and new opportunities of service. Kindle our hearts in fellowship with those of a cheerful countenance, and soften our hearts with sympathy for those who sorrow and suffer. Help us to maintain the honor of the Corps untarnished and unsullied and to show forth in our lives the ideals of West Point in doing our duty to Thee and to our Country. All of which we ask in the name of the Great Friend and Master of all.

Amen

The honor code is a little bit shorter, and slightly easier to memorize:

A cadet will not lie, cheat, steal, or tolerate those who do.

Religious beliefs aside, the themes and guidelines found in that Cadet Prayer struck a deep chord in me. Long before I found God

80

in my life in any deeply personal way, I turned to those words for guidance. When I think of those words—*a cadet will always choose the harder right instead of the easier wrong . . . a cadet will have the cheerful countenance . . . a cadet will never tolerate a half-truth when the whole truth can be won*—that's how I've tried to live my life at every turn.

A leader has to have a foundation to stand on. There has to be a moral code, a standard of principle from which he or she will not turn. West Point gave me a head start on building that foundation.

And the honor code, to me, is simply a matter of black and white—there are no shades of gray when it comes to honor. "A cadet will not lie, cheat, steal, or tolerate those who do." That's how I've lived my professional life at every turn. I think it's just as important to say, "A *leader* will not lie, cheat, steal, or tolerate those who do." In fact, imagine how quickly we could turn Washington around if we swore our leaders to that code! What I ask myself often is, "Why *wouldn't* our leaders want to lead with that kind of honor?"

There are plenty of delicate and difficult situations you face as a commissioned officer, and I faced my share from Fort Hood to Bosnia to Baghdad and back. Along the way I realized that the honor code, which was important to me as a cadet, was just as important if not *more* important to me as a professional officer. It is an absolute cornerstone of my foundation, and in many ways it signifies the essence of what I am—perhaps because it was driven home so forcefully.

I was at West Point during one of the more difficult moments in the school's history. A moment when the honor code itself was put to the test. My class, the class of 1977, was at the center of the 1976 cheating scandal.

A professor in the department of electrical engineering noticed that one student had received "help" on a series of take-home problems that were supposed to be done individually. He then looked a little closer at some of the other students' papers, and realized that answers on many of them were too similar to have come from original work. In the end, 117 students were turned in under suspicion of cheating.

As you might imagine, the scandal rocked West Point to its very core. The ramifications of this thing spread all over, as parents, the press, even Congress reacted.

Sid Berry, the superintendent of the Academy at the time, formed an internal review panel consisting of three full colonels and two cadets to investigate the allegations.

I was one of those two cadets.

In my particular company, Company A-2, there weren't any indications of cheating. Since I had established myself as a leader within that company, I was in a good position to judge fairly as far as Sid Berry was concerned. I can honestly say that I had no knowledge of any cheating across any of the companies before the scandal broke, and to say I was shocked by it is an understatement.

As a part of this panel, we would look at every single allegation to determine how expansive this potential problem was, and then make determinations about what we should do about it. We fed our findings and recommendations not only to General Berry, but to General Walt Ulmer, who was the commandant of cadets—and who would become a friend and mentor to me in the years following.

Here's where this process got tough.

I think most people know what kind of bonds and friendships are formed during your college years. At West Point those bonds are amplified. In most cases you stay with one company your entire time as a cadet. You go through Beast Barracks together, through Plebe Year together, you form relationships, and those relationships carry you through the rest of your life. But what we found in some companies is that those bonds had become so close that they had crossed the line into routinely violating the cadet honor code—as if the bond of friendship somehow overrode the honor system we had in place.

The fact is, other than that code, there was nothing keeping cadets from cheating. You could cheat if you wanted to cheat. You had access to folks who had already taken the same test you were about to take. The honor code demanded not only that you *not* cheat, but also that you would not tolerate those who do.

Some of the cheating was so blatant that kids had copied each other's work verbatim—going so far that when one kid doodled on his page during the test, the kids who copied it went ahead and copied the doodle, too (perhaps being foolish, or perhaps thinking it was a part of the answer). Other cases involved students simply talking about the test, or talking about the answers, when they shouldn't have been talking at all. And in some cases, a few of my classmates wound up being expelled from the school not because they themselves had cheated, but because they knew about the cheating and didn't report it as they were bound by the honor code to do.

They were found guilty of violating the honor code because they tolerated other cadets who broke the code.

This is a difficult thing for me to think back on, even today. Put yourself in their shoes: If you had been in a company that had been together for three years, if you did not cheat personally but knew that your best friend, the guy you'd been through Beast Barracks and Plebe Year and Yearling with, had cheated, you were supposed to turn him in. That's what the honor code says you are supposed to do, right? Would you have done it? Some folks chose not to do that, and as a result of not turning in their buddy they were found guilty, and action was taken.

I thank God that I wasn't confronted with that decision myself. I was oblivious to anybody cheating, so I wasn't faced with what is—as far as I can tell—the closest thing there is to a gray area in the honor code. In my work life, my adult life, or my professional life, if I discovered a co-worker cheating, lying, or stealing—I don't think I'd have much hesitation at all in turning that person in to the proper authorities, or dealing with the situation in whatever the most appropriate manner might be. But in school? If my best friend had cheated and I was aware of it back then, would I have turned him in? I've asked myself that question often over the last thirty-five years, and I'm still not sure of the answer. That's the hard truth. I'm not sure. Being an eyewitness to the West Point cheating scandal taught me important lessons about honor and the ramifications of breaking the code of honor. It helped heighten my awareness of the right and wrong in just about every decision I would face. This was an important moment for me morally, but it would be more than a decade before my moral compass would find its true north in the church.

After Sarah and I married in 1982, we became what I would call "recreational Christians." We went to church basically because everybody else did. It was a social place, a place to find community. Sarah had been baptized as a child, but not me. I was still very much the outsider, listening, maybe absorbing a lesson now and then, but not really understanding or even seeking to understand.

That all changed in 1988.

I was stationed at Fort Leavenworth, Kansas, when I first met a chaplain named Joe Miller. Joe Miller had a way of talking to a congregation that I'd never experienced before. Direct. Honest. Down-to-earth might be the best way to describe his oratory style.

I was thirty-two years old, and for the first time in my life, I guess I was ready to truly listen. One day, Joe stood up in front of our church and gave a talk about something called "inner peace." He quoted from the Bible, referring to Philippians 4:6–7: "Do not be anxious about anything, but in every situation, by prayer and petition, with thanksgiving, present your requests to God. And the peace of God, which transcends all understanding, will guard your hearts and your minds in Christ Jesus."

I admit I was anxious about a lot of things in those days: my career, my finances, my kids. That's pretty common for a lot of thirty-two-year-old men, I suppose. So the idea he presented of *not* being anxious about anything certainly resonated with me. That evening at the dinner table, my wife and I got to talking about the whole notion, and we realized that neither of us had that "inner peace" in our lives that Joe had spoken about. It was something we both simultaneously felt we were missing and ought to pursue.

We wound up working with Joe Miller intensely for the next six weeks, and Joe helped bring us to Christ. At the end of those six weeks, I was baptized. And even though Sarah had already been baptized as a child, she was baptized again—and I was able to participate in that.

I won't go on too long about this. I realize this decision belonged to my wife and me as individuals, and not everyone believes that church is for them. My own father, who is still with us, refuses to attend church to this day. He still takes the Lord's name in vain, and it drives me nuts! But I do believe a relationship with God is important—even if it has little to do with what church you belong to. And that relationship is certainly an important part of my life.

Ever since I was baptized at age thirty-two, I've started each day in prayer. I've dedicated some time each day to Bible study. I believe what it says in Joshua 1:8: "Keep this Book of the Law always on your lips; meditate on it day and night, so that you may be careful to do everything written in it. Then you will be prosperous and successful." And I've done my best to live my life as an honest reflection of my faith.

Even though I had tried to live my life with honor since my West Point days, it was Joe Miller who truly drove home the notion of lifestyle evangelism to me. "Hey, you can't be a sit-on-the-sidelines Christian," he would say. "You've got to be a lifestyle evangelist."

He's not the only person I had heard that from. When I was a brigade commander at Fort Hood, Texas, I was fortunate enough to bring Dallas Cowboy Coach Tom Landry in for a luncheon. He drove all the way from Austin, and we had about five hundred people come out to see him, thinking they were going to hear from Landry the coach. Instead, we heard from Landry the Christian. He told that group, "Being a Christian isn't about who you are. It's about what you do."

It was reinforcement from an unexpected place. And I've got to tell you, that notion has stuck with me ever since.

One of my favorite books is *A Life That God Rewards* by Bruce Wilkinson, and its basic message is this: God really doesn't care how many stars you wear or how much money you make; He cares about how many people you touch. That's how I want to live and how I've tried to live in my life of service in the United States military. And this conviction remains in my post-military career and will remain until the day I die.

My strength comes through my relationship with God. When I have difficult times, the first thing I do is drop to my knees and pray, "God, get me through these difficult times." I turn to Scripture, including 2 Timothy 3:16, 1 John 8:10, Psalm 119:11 (see appendix 2 for full texts), and more.

You will see reflections of my faith and a few more Scripture references in the coming chapters, as I tell you about some of the most difficult times I've faced as a leader, and how I got through them—finding opportunities in obstacles and adapting in the face of sometimes unimaginable pressures and difficulties.

My faith is the foundation on which I build my life. And as a leader, I hope you will take the time to ask yourself: *What is the foundation upon which I build my own life?*

11

The Captain and the Ship

I was awarded the Soldier's Medal in Camp Doha, Kuwait, at the end of the first Gulf War. For those of you who don't know, the Soldier's Medal is the highest award you can receive in peacetime for heroism. It's like the peacetime version of the Medal of Honor, and to get the medal you have to risk your own life to save others.

I tell this story not to be boastful, but to highlight my commitment to my subordinates, and my commitment to being a leader in the fullest sense of the word. I also hope to get you thinking about your own level of commitment—to ponder what you would do in a similar situation, as a reflection of just how much you care about the people you're leading; the people who are looking to you to lead.

It was 1991. I was the executive officer of this regiment, as a major, which means I was second-in-command of a unit of about 5,500 people. The war was over. We had sent Saddam Hussein's Republican Guard running back over the borders toward Baghdad, but had decided as a nation not to pursue them into Iraq. Since Saddam still had a viable army, my regiment remained as basically the last remaining American presence in the desert.

As a matter of organization at that time, we had asked and been given permission to consolidate all of our ammunition and vehicles together in one secure location. We basically collected a whole regiment's worth of trucks, tanks, and ammo that had been fanned out across the desert and put them in what amounted to a massive parking lot surrounded by a ten-foot concrete retaining wall.

One day, the aide to the one-star general called me and said, "Hey, we think you have a problem in your motor pool." There was black smoke rising from one of the vehicles.

The regiment's commander was out checking training, which meant the responsibility for whatever this was fell on my shoulders. We weren't under attack. I knew that. We were far from the enemy. So I hoped it was nothing as I got in my vehicle with my driver, Pete Bazek, and went down there. That's when I saw it: a fire in the engine compartment of one of our artillery vehicles. That might not have been much of a problem at all—if that vehicle weren't chock-full of ammunition and parked smack-dab in the middle of a tightly confined parking lot full of other vehicles full of ammunition.

Clearly I had to act fast. There was no time to call for help. No time to order someone else to do what had to be done. I crawled inside the vehicle and tried to put out the flames myself, but the fire was spreading too fast and the vehicle started blowing up around me. I made a decision then and there to evacuate the motor pool. As disciplined as our soldiers are, any emergency evacuation will result in a bit of chaos. It's to be expected. So during those frantic seconds of the evacuation, fifty-two of my soldiers were injured—not from the flames, and not from the horror of what was about to happen, but because they had to get over that ten-foot retaining wall in a hurry. And they did.

As the flames spread and the first sparks of ammunition fired off in the back of that artillery vehicle, I quickly exited out of the vehicle and started running toward the retaining wall. Unfortunately, the wall was too far away to reach in time. I was stuck in the middle of that motor pool when, all at once, the artillery vehicle exploded—causing all of the other vehicles and ammunition around me to catch fire and explode as well.

The engine access panel from that vehicle blew straight up in the air when it happened, landing with a crash within two feet of my head. Shrapnel flew everywhere, and yet, as I raised my head and picked myself up from the dirt, unable to hear anything but a high-pitched ringing that seemed to emanate from somewhere deep inside my brain, I knew I was okay. Somehow, by the grace of God, I had survived. And I knew what I had to do next.

I spent the next six hours rushing from vehicle to vehicle looking for those men who didn't evacuate or didn't have time to evacuate and were hiding. My mission was to find them and lead them to safety. I would not stop until I knew every one of those men was accounted for.

Six hours later, they were.

About $52 million worth of equipment was destroyed during that six-hour burn, including four M1-A1 battle tanks that were melted into useless hunks of molten steel. That's how horrendous the heat was. But no lives were lost. That's what mattered most.

As for the risk to my own life? Put it this way: I was in charge. In the face of disaster, if that meant I would go down with the proverbial ship, then so be it. As long as my crew was safe.

That's what a leader does. Or perhaps more accurately: That's who a leader *is*.

I can't say where all leaders get their strength when it comes to life-or-death situations. But the reason I was comfortable staying in that motor pool until everyone was safe is simply because I believed that God was going to protect me. I prayed and knew that if God wanted me to die that day, I would die; if He wanted to protect me, He would protect me. So I went about my business and that was that.

There, and in my multiple tours in Iraq, I was never once afraid of dying. Strong Christians, candidly, are not afraid of dying—they just don't want to do it anytime soon.

There's a book called *Heaven Is for Real*, which became a massive international bestseller when it was released, and with good reason. It tells the story of a four-year-old boy who underwent emergency surgery and hovered near death at a hospital, only to be revived and come back filled with stories of what heaven looked like, including unimaginably accurate details of the people he saw there during his brief visit to the afterlife. He knew things about people he had never known or been told about in life. Some critics have questioned whether the book could possibly be true, but I read it, and I believe everything that's in that book because it's based on the Bible. I believe that when you die you go to heaven and you leave behind your earthly trials and tribulations; you're there for all eternity. So I was never once afraid for my personal well-being, even when I was getting shot at all the time.

In Iraq, more than a decade after that motor pool incident, many times when my helicopter flew, it got shot at. I had the best helicopter pilots in the division, so through the 624 hours I spent in the back of a Blackhawk during combat operations, I never once sat back there worried. I figured if it was my time, it was my time.

I wasn't looking forward to dying. I wasn't hoping to die. But I was prepared to die—and my wife and children were prepared for that potential as well, even though none of us wanted it to happen.

Perhaps it takes a certain fearlessness to truly lead. If you have no faith, I'm not sure where that fearlessness can come from. In fact, a lady came up to me recently after one of my speeches and asked, "If my son doesn't have the strength that you profess, where is he going to get his strength from?" I confess that I really don't know the answer to that question.

Outside of my faith, I think that fearlessness I exhibited in Kuwait just comes from the notion of loving your subordinates like you love your own children. If your own children were caught in a fiery deathtrap, you'd do anything you could to save their lives. Back in Kuwait, I saw those men as my children. I made sure they were safe. Nothing could have stopped me. End of story. Staying behind and doing the right thing for my men was an easy decision to make.

Chances are the decisions you make in corporate America are not going to be life-or-death decisions, but leading from that same point of view will make a difference—because every decision you make as a leader does have an impact on people's livelihoods. If you make a bad decision, people could ultimately lose their jobs. Lost jobs can result in people being unable to pay their bills, having their homes foreclosed on, or not being able to send their kids to college. Is that what you would want for your own children? Whether their lives are on the line in the heat of the moment or not, you hold those lives in your hands.

So you have to ask yourself: Where do you get your source of strength as you're looking to take care of your subordinates? Do you have the faith to make it through the fire, for their sake? When the chips are down, when the motor pool's blowing up around you, when you're put to the test, will you have the strength to stand up and do what's right, based on the priorities that matter most?

In life, you never know when you'll be tested. I never could have foreseen the lengths to which I would be tested that day in 1991. And regardless of the fact that General Norman Schwarzkopf flew in to personally pin that medal on my uniform, I am simply humbled and thankful that neither my life nor any of my subordinates' lives were taken away that day. And I stand proud knowing that I did the right thing under the toughest of circumstances—knowing full well that I would do it all over again if I was faced with a similar challenge tomorrow.

12

Time Management

Before you get scared off, let me remind you that being a lifestyle evangelist doesn't mean you have to necessarily risk life and limb for your subordinates. In fact, I pray you never find yourself in a situation anything like the one I faced in Kuwait.

Most of the time, being a lifestyle evangelist just means sticking to your principles, and perhaps showing a little tough love when necessary—especially when it comes to leading by example in the discipline of time management, a crucial area of focus for this fast-paced, over-burdened world.

I firmly believe that the difference between an extremely successful individual or organization and a moderately successful one is time management. The reason? Without time management, organizations flounder. I think most business courses will teach you that. I think most managers and business leaders understand that. But the part that often gets overlooked is that without proper time management, the individual members of any organization can be consumed and overwhelmed by their work. And if the individuals who make up an organization are overwhelmed and consumed by their work, they are either going to burn out or stop working to their full capacity. And if the members of an organization are not contributing at their full potential, that will, by definition, negatively affect the organization.

It all comes down to taking care of your people. Take care of them, and they will take care of you.

We all need to find a level of work-life balance that works for us. That includes both leaders and subordinates. For all the talk about work-life balance and the almost mythical achievement it seems to be in the eyes of so many individuals who are aimlessly searching for it, there really is just one key: time management. I've enjoyed the benefits of work-life balance for the last twenty or more years in my career. How did I get there? By applying time management principles to my standard workweeks back home, as well as in the middle of combat operations in Iraq. I simply made time management a top priority, and that opened the door to the balance I needed.

You have to ask yourself: How much time do I need? Where can I carve out time not just for my work life, but also for my family life, my play life, and just for myself? Carving out time just for yourself is especially important for leaders. If a leader isn't having fun, nobody's having fun. Making time to let loose, to play, to enjoy yourself and relax will have a positive effect on you and the lives you influence. But there's another reason, too: As a leader, with so many people in your ear and so many decisions to make, you have to make time for yourself just to think. Whether I was working in division command, corps command, Installation Management Command, or in the university system after leaving the army, I've always carved out time on a daily basis just to think. Often it happened in the early hours of the morning when I was sure no one else would bother me.

─────────────────── REMINDER ───────────────────

HAVE FUN!

"If the boss ain't happy, ain't nobody happy!"

The block of time that worked for me was between four and six thirty every morning. For twenty years that was my quiet time. It may seem extreme to rise so early, but it worked for me. The phone's not ringing, my wife's asleep, nobody's asking me any questions—it was a time for me to read reports, write letters, plan for the day, or simply to think. If you don't make time to think, whatever decisions you make over the course of the day are just going to be echoing somebody else's thoughts, not yours. Over the last twenty years, this is the way my day started, even in my post-military career—it's me in the office, the dogs by my side on the floor, my wife and kids still sound asleep. When you find something that works for you, stick with it.

At any army base, PT (physical training) begins at 6:30 a.m., so that was how I marked the beginning of my workdays. Generally I was at work every day from 6:30 a.m. to 5:30 p.m. At 5:30 I'd head home for dinner and stay focused on the family until nine or so, when my kids (when they were younger) would head to bed. Then Sarah would do her thing, and I could work some more if necessary in preparation for the next day before going to bed myself. When the kids were up later, I'd remain focused on the family later. It evolved over time, and I had the freedom to evolve within a time structure I set for myself early on.

The rule I tried to follow was 15-7-2.

The 7 refers to sleep. You need to get seven hours of sleep. I certainly do. Everybody knows their own rhythms, but I don't function well on less than seven hours. I'm also a morning person. Some people aren't.

The 2 refers to physical training. I found, after a few years of trial-and-error and following other people's schedules and routines, that I've got to get seven hours of sleep and two hours of physical training in every day to keep my metabolism rate and my heart rate up—so I feel good enough to function at maximum capacity all day long.

That then leaves me the 15—fifteen hours a day for everything else.

In combat, it was pure 15-7-2: a full fifteen-hour workday, balanced by seven hours of sleep and two hours of working out. (Yes,

I worked out even in combat, which gave me the physical capability to have the endurance I needed to make it through each day. I couldn't risk not working out and seeing my muscles atrophy when I needed them most.)

And, by the way, I demanded that my subordinates follow a similar schedule. I needed them to be just as fit and efficient as I was in order for our organization to work.

Back home, that fifteen hours got broken into ten hours of work and five hours with the family. And the only reason I could pull that off was because of effective time management—including the managing of my subordinates' time at work.

Here's where the importance of time management comes within your organization. If you're organization isn't managing time effectively, it will drain time from other important areas of your life. And that's when work-life balance gets lost.

Don't Miss Out on Your Life

I'm pretty sure I first learned the importance of time management from Walt Ulmer, the West Point leader who would become a friend and one of the five big mentors in my career. (I'll talk more about my mentors, and the importance of mentorship, in part 3 of this book.)

Walt Ulmer had one particularly effective rule that I just flat-out copied, called "The 7-minute Rule." Basically, what I tell my subordinates in every setting I've ever worked in is that if we have a meeting that's supposed to start at 1:00 p.m., and it's 1:07 p.m. and I'm still not there, you all leave. I'm an effective time manager, so if I'm not there then obviously I've been sidetracked by something important, and I don't want you wasting your time waiting on me.

Whenever I communicated this for the first time in any new leadership role, people didn't believe me! They worried they'd somehow get in trouble for leaving, when in fact the last thing I wanted was for anyone to be sitting around twiddling their thumbs. The fact is, I would not be late if I could have been on time. I showed that by repeatedly being on time. This is a simple but effective way to walk the talk. But there were times when I didn't have a choice, and if I were sidetracked by something I could not avoid, it made no sense for me to keep people waiting. That's simply not a good use of their time.

Conversely, I make it very clear how important it is that everyone arrives at a meeting on time. There have been numerous cases when I'd walk into the conference room on time and lock the door—leaving people on the other side of the door wishing they'd been on time—just to demonstrate the importance of being on time.

West Point generally taught you that "on time" meant ten minutes early. That's what "on time" looks like to me. I realize not everyone operates by the same clock, but in the workplace, we need to. The fact is, in the modern world, just about every one of us carries a synchronized clock in our pocket. It's called a cell phone. So there is no excuse; you show up on time. Period. Otherwise you're wasting other people's time and slowing down their productivity.

(A side note here: In private life it's not always that easy, and sometimes you have to adjust accordingly. If you're married to a person like Sarah, you're dealing with a different perception of time management. She tends to always be fifteen minutes late even when I'm trying to be ten minutes early, so it's a game we play. If I know we've got to be ready at 1:00 p.m., I tell her we've got to be ready at 12:45. I build that into our schedule.)

In addition to arriving on time, I end meetings on time. If a meeting is supposed to end at 2 p.m., it ends at 2 p.m.—regardless of whether we're finished with the conversation. Once everyone in your organization knows that, and knows that they can't get away with belaboring a point or over-stretching a presentation, they all start watching the clock and using their time more effectively. When that clock struck 2, they knew I'd be standing up and saying my good-byes as I headed off to tackle the next block in my schedule. And while it may come off as a bit anal-retentive, showing your work force that discipline is extremely powerful.

I did hurt some people's feelings when I locked them out of the room or cut off the discussion rather than let the meeting run over. But they knew I was doing it for the sake of time management, and they knew I was doing it so that I could indeed live my life the way I described to them from day one: so I could be home for dinner by 6 p.m., and so they could be home for dinner by six, too.

I carried that "home-for-dinner" rule into every position I held in my career, including my work at the Pentagon overseeing the management of every army installation on earth. I refused to sacrifice my family time for my work time, or my workers' family time, either—and in the end, that was appreciated. I walked the walk. I lived by my words, and I acted upon them. I was never one of these bosses who would hold a long meeting promoting work-life balance, and then make everybody stay at work until 9:00 p.m. because of some big deadline that same week. (If you're working in corporate America, I have a feeling that sounds all too familiar to you!) My workers knew where I stood and respected it because I lived by it. Therefore, I got results.

You may disagree with the way I organize meetings or stick to a firm timetable. The point is, I walked the walk that I said I wanted others to walk. I demonstrated the importance of time management in my daily life, and I was able to take care of my jobs and my family at the same time as a result of that effort.

Despite the extreme nature of my career in the military, I didn't miss my son's football games or my daughter's plays unless I was deployed—unless I was physically gone. And unlike travel in corporate America, my deployments were compulsory. When I was forced to go to Kosovo, it wasn't a choice. When I was forced to go to Baghdad, it wasn't a choice.

I meet CEOs all the time who miss big life events in their families. And it always saddens me, because I know that it doesn't have to be that way. They have a choice. They have a choice to be better time managers, and to give the time they need to their families if they want to. And if you've been listening to me, you understand why I think that's important.

I do my best to explain this to people all the time, and sometimes I wish everybody would just listen to more country-western music. There are so many lessons in those lyrics. There's a song out called

"Don't Miss Your Life" by a guy named Phil Vassar. It's the story of a corporate executive flying from one place to another, and there's an old man sitting next to him, and he says he's off to another meeting and it's his daughter's birthday, and the old man warns him about the regrets he has from his own successful career: how he missed his daughter's first steps and his son's crossing home plate for the first time. He tells the young executive, "Don't miss your life."

I put it another way when I talk to groups of people all over this country: "Don't miss your dash."

You see, when you pass by a cemetery, you notice that just about every headstone has a birth date and a death date, and those two dates are separated by a dash. That dash represents your life. What you do with that life is up to you. Believe me, you don't want to miss it.

In the army there were no ifs, ands, or buts: When I had to go, I had to go. And that time away, when I couldn't dedicate my allotted hours to my family, was extremely tough on me.

Funny enough, the bulk of my time away did start with a choice. My family was in Texas when the army first decided to send me to Washington, D.C. My daughter, Susan, was going into her junior year of high school. I thought I would only be spending fourteen months in Washington, and we sat down as a family and decided it would be too disruptive to the family to move everyone for a fourteen-month stay. So I went to D.C. by myself, and commuted back and forth for as much family time as I could get.

It was tough, but we made it through. And the effort I made putting all those hours on planes back and forth was worth every added stress to my time-management plans, for sure.

But then I got promoted to general officer and wound up staying in D.C. for two years. When I finally came back home, the army deployed me to Kosovo for a year—just as my son was entering his senior year. (My kids are just twenty-two months apart in age.) I missed too many of his football games because of that. I missed too many of those little moments in the afternoon when I could have helped him with his homework. I missed those moments sitting around the dinner table with him as he finished his high school career.

The army wound up sending me to Italy after that, and then off to Iraq—back-to-back-to-back. That time lost with my son had a cost.

I missed my son's high school graduation because I was in Naples, Italy. I simply didn't have a choice, and of course my son didn't blame me for that. We were an army family. We knew absences sometimes came with the territory. But I didn't realize how emotional it was for Lucas until one day a few years later he said, "Dad, it really hurt me that you weren't there for my high school graduation." He didn't blame me—but that didn't mean it didn't hurt.

My daughter graduated from college in four years, but for my son, it took eight years. I think it was partly because I wasn't there to help him. Right then and there, as we talked, I committed to be the guest speaker at his college graduation. When he did finally graduate, not only was I there speaking, I was the one who got to hand him his diploma. At the end, I was finally *there*.

The thing is, you never get those moments back.

No matter how big or important the organization is that you're leading, your life and your family are bigger. Time management, focused on the priorities that you set, is the key to your being a part of your own life.

Don't miss your dash, people. Use your time wisely. And make sure your work force follows your lead. They'll thank you for it in the end.

REMINDER

ACHIEVE A WORK-LIFE BALANCE.

"How are you living your dash?"

13

Focus Management

While I credit time management with much of my success as a leader, and my adherence to time management as a prime example of how I've tried to behave as a lifestyle evangelist, I think my ability to focus comes in a close second.

I think as a culture, and certainly as a country, we've all become too easily distracted from the tasks at hand. A little distraction now and then is somewhat understandable, but the worst part about what I see happening today is that the culprits, in most cases, aren't even worthwhile distractions. Instead, we're consumed by what I call "absurd distractions." (Thomas Friedman refers to this idea in his book, *That Used to Be Us*.)

Think about our political landscape. Rather than focus on critical issues such as the deficit, unemployment, or our heavy reliance on foreign oil, our politicians are constantly focused on things that are absolutely absurd. Just one month before the 2012 presidential elections, all focus suddenly turned to Big Bird and whether we should cut the miniscule funding we give to PBS.

There was a time not long ago, in this post-9/11 world, when Congress couldn't pass a basic budget let alone any major bill, but somehow managed to pass a bill regulating the audible volume of television commercials. How does that take precedence over, well, just about anything else? Or the absurd distraction I had to work around during my time at the Pentagon: revoking the military's Don't Ask, Don't Tell policy. We were fighting two wars at the time. Two! I remember sitting in the Pentagon as we're trying to figure out how to fight these wars in Iraq and Afghanistan with limited resources, and then all of a sudden, for political reasons, we decide to announce that we're going to revoke Don't Ask, Don't Tell. This distraction was all anyone could talk about, from the evening news to the offices of the top brass, from the White House down to the dinner tables of soldiers and their families. I'm not saying these are issues that don't deserve being addressed at some point, but in the context of the crises that are enveloping our nation, they are absolutely absurd distractions.

We all can recognize absurd topics that are occupying our minds, we just choose not to do anything about them. I mean, everywhere you go, the water-cooler talk has been taken over by the Kardashians (*who?*) or which celebrity marriage is falling apart. And it's one thing to gossip at work, but when the gossip is all about the lives of so-called reality TV stars, there's clearly a national problem with our ability to focus on the real world.

Even in the business world the distractions are never ending. In the summer of 2012, one guy from Chick-fil-A announced where he stood on the gay marriage issue, and he had the mayors of Boston and Chicago and elsewhere come out and lambast him for expressing his opinion. Suddenly it was all the media was talking about. Thousands of people were boycotting Chick-fil-A, and thousands more came out and protested the boycotts! A restaurant best known for their fried chicken sandwiches with the pickle on top was now the center of too many people's attention. And yet there's no uproar, no protest, no support shown over life-and-death issues that are staring us in the face. This is the very definition of an absurd distraction. And when the media and mayors and everyone else are focused on something so absurd, you can bet they're not focusing on the stuff that really matters.

My point is, you cannot focus on critical issues when you're consumed by absurd distractions.

It is up to you, as a leader, to take charge and tell your work force what to focus on. To actually say, "Here's what you've got to focus on. We're not going to allow ourselves to be distracted by all these other things"—no matter how much distraction and how much pressure you're under to do otherwise.

Perhaps my biggest test of focus came when President Bush announced the surge in Iraq back in 2007.

To refresh your memory, the war in Iraq had been stretching on since March of 2003. The war was incredibly unpopular at that point: We had lost a lot of American lives for what seemed like fairly dubious reasons, and as far as the American people were concerned, this war had no end in sight.

I'm not going to get into the arguments about whether we should have invaded Iraq in the first place. That discussion is for a different book. We were there. We had a job to do—and it was pretty clear to everyone involved that we weren't doing the job the way it needed to be done.

From the very beginning of this war, we in the army knew that we didn't have enough troops on the ground to tackle the tasks at hand. We had enough troops to get in, defeat Saddam Hussein, and get out. But that wasn't what we were tasked with accomplishing. There was a counterinsurgency at play. There was rebuilding to do. Our military was tasked with what should have been State Department work, with aid work, with peace-keeping, and policing work in a country fraught with ethnic conflicts of epic proportions.

In that regard, despite the many calls for us to simply get out and bring our troops home, a massive surge of troops was just what that war needed. It was a good decision under the circumstances—and one that should have come much sooner, in my opinion. But there was just one hitch now that the surge was finally hatched: the rapid speed of troop deployment.

I was in charge of the army's Third Infantry Division at that time, and by January we had already been planning to deploy to Iraq. The plan was this: We would have six months to train and prepare for a rebuilding mission in the northern part of the country. Well, you know what they say about the best-laid plans. That January I got a call from General Ray Odierno, who was the corps commander in Iraq at that time.

"Hey, Rick," he said, "don't think about coming in six months— think about coming in six weeks." *Six weeks?*

He wasn't through: "And don't think about going north," he said, "think about going south."

With President Bush's announcement, our six-month timetable was shortened to six weeks, and our plan to go on a rebuilding mission in northern Iraq was completely scrapped. The new mission? I would be placing my 25,000 soldiers into combat operations in a highly dangerous area just south of Baghdad known (for good reason) as the Triangle of Death.

The American army has the ability to adapt. We've built massive amounts of flexibility into our operations and into our people; I'll talk more about what it takes to create an adaptable work force in part 4 of this book.

So the biggest challenge I faced in preparing an entire division—including our division headquarters—to dive into a combat operation in the most dangerous part of Iraq on a six-week timetable, was to keep everyone on-task and focused on what needed to be done. No distractions.

With a truncated timetable and such a serious and daunting task in front of us, the absurd distractions went out the window pretty easily. There's nothing to eliminate foolishness and get you down to basics quite like facing the prospect of enemy fire in a foreign land. But there are also all sorts of distractions that set in when your organization is challenged—including the distraction of naysayers.

There were a number of people on my staff who reacted to that six-months to six-weeks news by shutting down.

"General," they said, "there's no way we can make such a major shift in that amount of time! You've got to call someone! You've got to tell them we can't do it!"

They immediately gave up. There are certain people in any organization who are so uncomfortable working outside of their current planning process that when someone throws them a curve ball, they immediately shut down. And that shutting down keeps anything from happening. It's up to a leader to point them in the right direction, to reassure them, and to show them that it can be done.

One of the reasons some of my staff shut down was because the army had given us so many tasks to accomplish before we deployed—a number that could not physically be tackled in six weeks. The fact was, the army had given my division headquarters 137 tasks to complete before we deployed. Those tasks included advanced training exercises that had to be perfected, setting up command and control linkages between the various brigades that would report to us in the field, allocating all kinds of resources—from personnel to equipment to money, and more. My staff was right. We couldn't tackle 137 tasks in six weeks. It *was* impossible. But that wouldn't keep us from deploying on time. It simply meant that we had to focus—and that ability to focus fell squarely on my shoulders.

I asked myself, "Of those 137 tasks, which are the most critical?" I pared the list down to thirty-eight tasks, and I focused on those thirty-eight tasks during that six-week training period, while simultaneously working to develop a timeline in which we could tackle the rest.

"Which are the tasks that we have to do now? Which tasks can we accomplish on the fly, as we move? Which tasks can we work on after we arrive in the field?"

We would still get through the 137 tasks. They would just be done on a different timetable, and many of them would be done after we hit the ground in Iraq.

Presenting my staff with just thirty-eight tasks to tackle in six weeks suddenly made the job seem doable. I would still have to work to keep them focused, of course, so no one would be sidetracked into working on the remaining tasks until those thirty-eight tasks were completed. But by my trimming the tasks down to the absolute most critical, suddenly the six-week shift seemed like less of a crisis and more of an "urgent development."

Keep Your Eye on the Goal

In my early morning time, I looked ahead to the opening days of a major combat operation. *What would we need to know? What would likely happen?* For example: The air force would be heavily involved in bombing campaigns right from the outset, and in any heavy air operation, chances are we'd be tasked with downed aircraft recovery. My men needed to be ready for that. So that's one of the training exercises we tackled at home. And guess what? Within a week of our arrival that March, we faced a downed aircraft recovery mission—and my crew responded seamlessly.

Taking the time to think, taking the time to plan, taking the time I needed to lead with confidence rather than with urgency or panic made all the difference. I can't stress enough how important it is for leaders to decide when to decide. If you need to make a decision on the spot, that's one thing. But if you can take a few minutes, a few hours, a few days to decide, you need to set a timetable and stick to it. Use that time to consider your options thoroughly. But don't over-think. Sometimes too much information and weighing too many options can cause more confusion than clarity. Use your expertise, your experience, your faith, your knowledge, your beliefs, and your guiding principles to make your decisions, and then stick by them.

Listening to my gut, relying on my own expertise and experience in the field while culling suggestions from my staff and filtering them through my own thought process, allowed me to make a conscious decision to say, "This is where we're going to focus." And even though there were lots of other folks around me who were trying to distract me, running around like chickens with their heads cut off, yelling, "We've got to do this!" or "We've got to do that!" I kept the focus on the critical tasks.

In all walks of life, if leaders would focus on the critical tasks and not the absurd distractions, we would all be better off. (The media could learn that lesson, too!)

Some of you may argue with me about this, but I have to say that one of the biggest distractions we face in our home and family time is the constant draw of email and other after-hours office communications. It is my belief that you have to have the mental discipline to shut that communication down at certain times for your own sanity, and in the long run this will improve productivity. There are multiple studies out there that show how devastating a single email chime on your phone can be when it comes to affecting your focus. Every time it vibrates or beeps, you stop what you're doing and answer it. It then takes time—sometimes lots of time—to get back to whatever you were doing, whether it's writing a report or playing with your kid. And that's not good for anyone.

There are some bosses who demand instant responses, who expect their subordinates to be online and reachable at all hours of the day. That needs to change!

A boss who demands urgent replies to emails at all hours of the day or night, including the weekends, simply isn't operating efficiently. That boss isn't focused on the right things. If you've studied any managerial course work in the past, you've probably come across the Franklin Covey quadrants of productivity. I would say that boss is operating in quadrant 3, which is not where you want to be.

I'll paraphrase those quadrants here just to give you a better sense of what I mean. There are basically four quadrants your organization can operate in at any given time.

Quadrant 1 is when everything is urgent and everything's important. That's what it's like in the Pentagon, where everyone's rushing around from crisis to crisis and there isn't time to deal with anything else.

Quadrant 2 is when you're focused on what's important but not urgent—which means you actually have time to focus and make good decisions about all kinds of things.

Quadrant 3 is when everything's urgent, but none of it is important. That's the "let's set up a meeting to talk about the next meeting" world that so many corporations are stuck in.

Quadrant 4 is when nothing's urgent and nothing's important—which basically means you're spinning your wheels and not getting anything done.

Clearly quadrant 2 is where you want to spend most of your time and where you want your organization to spend most of its time no matter what it is you do for a living. Quadrant 2 is what happens when you focus and avoid unnecessary and especially absurd distractions. Quadrant 2 is achievable even when the pressure is on, as we proved by staying focused and on-task in the six-week preparation for the surge.

How do you get there? By asking the right questions and demanding the right answers. When it comes to keeping my organizations focused, the three questions I ask all the time are:

1. "Are we doing the right things?"
2. "Are we doing things right?"
3. "What are we missing?"

If you want to keep your organization focused on the right things, then those questions have to be asked repeatedly and answered repeatedly. I worked in a few areas and organizations where generally the answer to those first two questions was "no," but we went ahead and kept doing what we were doing anyway, often without any consideration of question number three. (The Pentagon certainly comes to mind here!)

As a leader, I've made it my mission to answer those questions honestly. Whether going into combat or just keeping your business afloat, you want to be able to answer those first two questions with a yes, and the final question with, "Nothing at all." That's how you'll know that you're focused on doing the right things, and doing the right things to stay focused.

--- R E M I N D E R ---

DECIDE WHEN TO DECIDE.

"Take the time to think."

14

Walking the Walk

Do you want to know one of the primary reasons I've been able to lead on my terms for the last twenty years—bucking convention, standing up for what I believe in, getting results, adapting at will, overcoming obstacles by turning them into opportunities, and never looking back while I climbed the ranks all the way to becoming a three-star lieutenant general in the United States Army? All while staying true to my personal mantra of putting God first, family second, and career third? I've been able to do that because I wasn't held back by the "A" word.

"What's the 'A' word," you ask?

Aspiration.

I know, I know. That sounds backwards. We've all been programmed to believe that aspiration is a positive thing; that aspiration is a motivator. And it is—to some degree. But drawing the line on reasonable aspirations can also give you a tremendous amount of freedom.

I know this because I accomplished my highest career aspiration all the way back in 1993.

Shortly after leaving West Point, I set one very particular goal for myself: I wanted to be a battalion commander. That was it. That was as high as I wanted to go in the army. Once I accomplished that goal, I convinced myself I would be satisfied with my career.

The army promoted me to Lieutenant Colonel Battalion Command in 1993. Everything after that was gravy. My time in the army was pure service after that. I wasn't aiming for another promotion, and that gave me a certain amount of latitude I hadn't had before. If I was faced with a bad boss who wanted me to do things that were counter to my beliefs, counter to putting God and family first, I had the latitude to just say no. If I couldn't have lived with a certain situation, I simply would have left the army and moved on to another career. I had already accomplished my goal. I had achieved my mark of success.

That gave me freedom to follow my mantra, and to spread my mantra to others.

Leaders have to set the precedent. You have to draw the line. You have to have your priorities in life. My relationship to God, family, and then profession—in that order—became my mantra. If I was told to do anything that violated those priorities, I just wouldn't do it. I was okay doing that because I had already become successful. And that gave me power.

Everybody can get to that place in their chosen profession, unless they've got an overly ambitious sense of aspiration. If you've got the sort of aspiration that causes you to do things you know you shouldn't do in order to get from here to there, that's an issue you've got to deal with personally. You have to ask yourself, "What is good enough?" when it comes to your career, and then balance that with the all-important question, "What's the most important thing in your life?"

For me, putting God and family ahead of my career was paramount. That was the key to "living my dash."

On your deathbed, you're not going to wish you had worked more. You're not going to wish that you had worked harder. You're going to wish that you had spent more time with your loved ones. If people can acknowledge that, then they're probably going to be better at the work-life balance.

Just to hammer this point home, I want to tell you about a town hall meeting I held with about five hundred staffers at Fort Leavenworth, Kansas, during my time as head of Installation Management Command (IMCOM)—overseeing a worldwide work force of 120,000 people, most of whom were civilians. Whenever I held a town hall meeting with these employees—and I did that as often as I could—I would talk about the importance of work-life balance. At this particular presentation, I spoke at length about living your dash, and how important it was to use time management to get your work done during the day and spend your evenings and weekends with your family. I explained to the audience that if you're not maintaining a work-life balance, you're working way too hard and sacrificing your family. "God didn't promise you tomorrow. He only promised you today—and that's why it's called 'the present,'" I said. "So you've got to reverse that behavior. You've got to focus on your family. You never know when it will be too late."

There happened to be a mother and her thirty-two-year-old daughter in the audience that day. They both worked in the same installation, and yet the two of them had indeed been so focused on work that they were never spending any time together. They had become estranged, even though they both lived there and worked together at Fort Leavenworth.

For some reason, on that particular day, my words got through to these two women. They approached me after the presentation was over and told me their story. That day they committed to spend more time with each other, to focus on each other more, to tell each other that they loved the other. I was humbled and thankful that my words could have some effect.

One week later, that thirty-two-year-old daughter died. She died of natural causes. It wasn't an accident, though there was no way to see it coming, no way to predict it. She just died.

To this day, that mother still contacts me now and then to say, "Thank you. Thank you for that one week."

I'll say it again, people: Live your dash. If you love somebody, pick up the phone and call that person and tell them that you love them.

If you've wronged somebody, go and fix that wrong. Don't assume you'll have another tomorrow to do that. Go do it today.

I'm thankful every day for the time I've been able to spend with my family, and that might never have been possible had I aspired to be a general. The fact that I kept my aspirations in check allowed me to live life on my terms—and, in an ironic twist, helped me climb the ladder of success even faster because I could walk the walk while standing on the solid foundation of my beliefs. Having the ability to do that made me capable of being a leader; of leading rather than following when it came to the principles I believe in.

I want to step back for a moment here, lest you think that I'm making myself out to be a little too perfect. The fact that I've been able to live out my own personal mantra, the fact that I have achieved what I consider to be a successful work-life balance, the fact that I've accomplished some great things and amassed a proud record of service to this country over the last thirty-five years doesn't mean I'm perfect. In fact, far from it. I think it's important that I share a bit about that here.

In the Bible, Paul says, "For I do not do the good I want to do, but the evil I do not want to do—this I keep on doing" (Romans 7:19). To paraphrase, Paul is basically asking a very poignant question of himself: "Why do I keep doing what I'm not supposed to do?"

I find myself asking that very same question all the time. As much as I try to walk the walk and live my life as an example to others, I do things that are 180 degrees different from what I preach. Sometimes so much so that I'm embarrassed by them.

On one hand, it's a good thing that I can acknowledge this. At least I know I'm screwed up! I tell people all the time, "If you're screwed up and you know it, you're less screwed up than if you're screwed up and don't know it."

But on the other hand, it can be frustrating and embarrassing, even if I can find strength in the Bible that allows me to chalk it up to being human. Romans 3:23 reminds me that "all have sinned and fall short of the glory of God."

I'll give you a couple of specific areas that always get me. The first one is anger management. I've been fighting anger management my whole life. I remember as a battalion commander (just after my highest aspiration was realized), one of my captains said something so unbelievably foolish that my reflex was to hit him! I knew better, of course, so rather than hit him, I hit the easel that I was using. I slammed that easel so hard that I dented it and busted my hand—and this was in front of my subordinates. It was a reflection of not being able to control my temper.

When I was a young captain, one of my soldiers aggravated me so badly that I actually took off my helmet and threw it against the armored-personnel carrier. I threw it so hard, I destroyed my helmet. Think about that for a second: This was a helmet. A solid apparatus meant to keep your head safe in combat. You've got to throw a helmet pretty hard in order to destroy it, but that's how mad I was!

I'm very conscious of the fact that on any given day I can flip. I can demonstrate absurd behavior. I'll do it at home sometimes, too—just get so mad about something that I lose it. So I'm conscious of that all the time. God wants you to control your anger. God doesn't want you to be an angry person. And it's certainly not "lifestyle evangelism" to be punching easels and destroying helmets. But it's hard to always stop and think, *Now, what am I demonstrating here?*

There's a phrase a lot of people use: "What would Jesus do?" That's in my mind all the time. But even Jesus got mad. There was a time he threw everything out of the temple! He got mad. And Paul—I like studying Paul, because he messed up all the time. That gives me hope.

Since that hand-busting moment in the early 1990s, I've mostly worked through that anger. I don't think there's a time since I was a flag officer through today that you'd find somebody who would say, "Hey, Lynch screamed at me," or "Lynch belittled me," or any of those kinds of responses. I've been able to acknowledge that I had that problem, and have worked on it. I do my best to live the example I want to set. But it hasn't been easy.

The second area I tend to come up short is swearing. It says in the Bible, "Don't use the Lord's name in vain." It also says, essentially,

"Don't swear. Don't use blasphemy. Don't curse." Putting the Bible aside, I think it's pretty important to demonstrate graciousness and a sense of control as a leader, and a foul mouth tends to show something that's just the opposite of that.

For me, especially since I've been trying to act as a lifestyle evangelist since I was thirty-two years old, staying true to the no-swearing rule is pretty important. Once again, though, I've been embarrassed by my own behavior while leading. The time it hit me hardest was, again, back when I was a battalion commander. In addition to trying to be the best lieutenant colonel I could be, I was attempting to be a decent spiritual leader to my subordinates (at least to those who were interested in some spiritual guidance). So I hosted prayer breakfasts and prayer lunches, and would bring soldiers and their families together to talk about their spiritual fitness. At the very end of my time, after serving as a battalion commander for two full years, the day before I left, a staff sergeant came up to me and said, "You're a hypocrite. You profess to be a man of faith and live a life like Jesus, but you swear like a sailor."

That was a real gut-shot for me. Nobody had ever confronted me on that, but he was exactly right. Here I was saying one thing but doing something else. The audio didn't match the video.

If you've been around a bunch of soldiers, or even seen a war movie or two, you probably have some idea just how much swearing goes on every minute of every conversation. It's par for the course. Here I was trying to set a higher example, yet falling prey to that loose language like everyone else. It was unbecoming of a leader, and from that point forward I did my best to stop it.

I fail. Almost every day. I find that swearing is a part of my natural cadence, especially when I get passionate about an issue or angry about something. So every day I struggle with it. I slip, even though I know I shouldn't. That's a frailty. I am a frail man, as are each one of us. We all sin and fall short of the glory of God, as it says in the book of Romans. But making a conscious effort, trying to do your best, trying to walk the walk and be conscious of the example you're setting for others is better than nothing, and I believe that the bar leaders set for themselves should be as high as possible if they're going to be successful.

Trying to walk the walk is better than not walking the walk at all.

And don't forget, all of this applies to your family life, too. The impact of the way you act and how you live stretches far and wide. Sometimes much further than you think.

My daughter, Susan, got engaged a while back. And you know what she told me one day? She said she learned how a woman should be treated in a relationship by watching the way I treated her mom as she was growing up. Watching our relationship taught Susan what to look for in her own relationships as she grew into the incredible adult she is today—and she said "yes" to a young man who treats her like gold.

She learned that by watching me! I didn't even realize she was paying attention. I wasn't purposefully trying to set an example. It's just the way it was. What would have happened had I been acting differently? What would have happened had I *not* shown my wife the love and respect she deserved, and that I wanted to give her? What would have happened had I worked all the time and not been home enough to give Susan any impression in that regard whatsoever?

That's emotional. That's powerful.

I made an impact on my daughter in an area where I wasn't even consciously trying to make an impact. I made an impact on one of the most important people in my life just by staying true to who I am.

As I think about that now, I can't help but think that that's what leadership is all about. At all levels.

Walking the walk is what matters the most.

15

Voice Amplification

With every promotion, with every rise through the ranks, with every new job title, your voice gets louder.

I didn't realize this fully until I became a general—and started seeing the reactions from my subordinates when they encountered the stars on my uniform.

There were times when I'd be having a conversation with one of our soldiers or officers, especially if it was about something critical, and they would perceive me as yelling at them (even though I wasn't even raising my voice). Yelling—something I almost never did after focusing on controlling my anger way back in the early '90s. After some further reflection, it occurred to me that the stars on my chest were acting as voice amplification devices.

Because of my position and the perceived power that comes with that position, every word I said had more of an impact. And that goes for anyone with any big title in any organization: CFO, CEO, president, vice president, senior manager, etc.

Knowing that you're speaking through an amplification system comes with a newfound responsibility. Consider this: If you were walking around in your everyday life with a headset microphone strapped on, like one of those things Garth Brooks wears in concert, knowing that every word that came out of your mouth was going to be heard by thousands of individuals, or at the very least blasted full-force at whoever was listening, would you think twice before you spoke? I have a feeling you would. When a leader speaks, there is a ripple effect. Your words have a way of not only getting amplified in the mind of whoever's listening, but also repeated, far and wide, throughout your organization and beyond.

That takes some getting used to, and a lot of leaders seem to either ignore that reality, or simply forget it. Sometimes, given the workload you face, the constraints on your time, the importance of the decisions you have to make every hour of every day, you can't always taper your tone. You can't always pause to make sure your amplified voice isn't too loud or too harsh. But most of the time? It's your duty as a leader to be aware of your amplification, to use it wisely, to use it sensitively, and to choose not to abuse it.

If you're aware that your words have greater impact because of your position, you can choose to use your words to get results. If you know that your workers are listening when you speak, because you truly care about them (as I've explained earlier, just as you would your own children), and knowing that they might even be a little afraid to cross you for fear of being yelled at (even if you never yell!), you can speak with a certain amount of confidence that whatever you say is going to get done.

Throughout my career I've held counseling sessions with my subordinates on a regular basis. I'll talk more about that in the next section of this book, but they were similar to what you might call an "employee review" in the corporate world. It's where I would have someone come in to go over their work, their progress, see how they're doing, and talk about their strengths and maybe the areas where they could use some improvement. And because I was doing that from a senior position, what I often found in the course of counseling is that when the people who were working for me truly believed that I cared, they would always feel bad if they let me down. My subordinates, countless times over the years, would modify their performance, improve what they were doing, and work harder because they didn't want to let me down.

When handled with care, that is the net effect of voice amplification. Your work force does a better job because they know it matters to you, and they can hear you loud and clear.

Unfortunately, being in a position of power and having that amplified voice can also leave your work force feeling like they're struggling to be heard. Sometimes they're left feeling like they're in the seventy-fifth row at that Garth Brooks concert, and they're trying to read Garth a private love note over the booming bass of the loudspeakers and the roar of the crowd. Your impact as a leader can be so great that sometimes your work force feels like an audience. And frankly, I'm embarrassed by that. I want my subordinates to feel important—because they are. And this is another one of those areas where I struggle. It's not an intentional thing, of course, but it's something I'm conscious of and would like to improve in myself.

I do command climate surveys all the time. That's basically a survey you use to ask the work force, "What's on your mind? How's it going?" I'll walk into a group of people and give them all a blank three-by-five card, and I'll say, "On the front side, write the three things you like most about this division, and on the back write the three things you like the least." It's anonymous, so I get good feedback that way.

In my last posting before I retired from the army, one area of concern came out loud and clear: My subordinates thought I was just too busy.

I really had three jobs during my final years in the army: I was the assistant chief of staff for installation management in the Pentagon, which was a full-time job; I was the commanding general of the Installation Management Command (IMCOM), which was another full-time job (and by the way, their headquarters were physically separated: IMCOM had a San Antonio headquarters, so I had to split my office time between Washington, D.C., and San Antonio); and then the chief of staff of the army had me run this thing called the Services and Infrastructure Core Enterprise. If you're going to run a large organization like IMCOM, overseeing business on 163 army bases around the world, with 120,000 people, you've got to run it like an enterprise, not like a series of stovepipes. So routinely I'd have to get the medical community, service providers, and engineers together to say, "Okay, what are we going to do on our installations to be able to accomplish what is needed at a reduced cost?" That, as you can imagine, was yet another full-time job.

With so much on my plate and so much to oversee, I didn't have any time to waste. As a result, I found myself being very curt with people. That's what came across loud and clear in those surveys: "Lynch doesn't seem to have any time for us because he's always got something else going on."

That embarrassed me. In reality, I had time for what mattered, but I didn't have time to waste. There was a communication breakdown between what I perceived to be giving the time I needed to give, and the time my work force thought they needed to have in order to be heard. That's not an easy thing to overcome, but here's how that breakdown happened and why that perception existed.

When I walk into a meeting, I'm the most prepared person in the room. The meeting's going to start on time, and it's going to end on time. There's going to be an agenda. There have been countless books on this, but hardly anyone seems to follow those guidelines. Ever.

I followed the guidelines. I walked the walk. My meetings would never last more than an hour, so I was going to be prepared. In order to do that, if you were set to give a presentation at that meeting, I insisted on seeing the slides you were going to show or any narrative you were going to read ahead of time. I would generally use my early morning time period, that 4:00 to 6:30 a.m. block in my schedule, to go over those slides and those notes to prepare for the meetings. That worked well for me, and it meant there wouldn't be any wasted time in those meetings.

The problem is, all these people worked so hard on their presentations, and they'd come into the meeting and want to work their way through the slides. Well, I don't need you to read the slides to me; I already read 'em! So I'd go into the meeting and say, "Get to slide twelve and tell me more about the third bullet point, because that's what I'm interested in." And frankly, that offended a lot of people. They put time into preparing the slide presentation and sought the opportunity to shine in front of the general. They felt let down or even angry if I didn't give them that opportunity to shine. I knew I had to get through the meeting because I had something else to do in the next block of time, and the next block after that. My days were scheduled from minute to minute most of the time.

That was a problem for me.

I tried really hard at the beginning of the meeting *not* to jump to the point I was most interested in. But when they'd get up there and start talking about stuff that I didn't want or need to hear, I'd have to jump in—"Okay, go to slide twenty-three . . ."—and I could tell that I had taken the wind out of their sails.

To say I regret that is probably too strong. It was what I needed to do. But it was something I was conscious of because I had an impact on people's lives. They didn't leave that meeting feeling good about what they had done. I felt good about the meeting because I got out of it what I wanted or needed, but I'm sure they didn't go home that night and tell their spouse and kids how much they enjoyed being able to present to the general.

As I've spent more time in corporate America as a consultant since leaving the army, I see that happening in boardrooms all over this country. That's what corporate leadership is doing to their work forces right now: They're taking the wind out of people's sails. They're so busy that they're not taking the time to listen when they already have what they need. And perhaps there needs to be some better balance here.

I don't have a pat answer for fixing this—other than making sure our leaders and managers aren't overburdened with too many jobs at once. But it is something I hope we can become more aware of and work on together.

Even when we don't have three full-time jobs, do any of us really have time for BOGSAT (the acronym for a Bunch Of Guys Sitting Around a Table) in the workplace? I sure don't. That's quadrant 3 activity—going to a meeting just to plan the next meeting. The fact is, a slide show shouldn't be about the act of the slide show. It should be about the content and important points in that slide show. And maybe that's the answer right there. Maybe PowerPoint is just an instrument of the devil!

I like people to leave a conversation with me feeling enriched, feeling like they were listened to, feeling like I truly cared—but sometimes I got so busy that I didn't do that very well. Of course, I was setting a good example by showing that I was going to do the work efficiently and get home to my family at six—so that they could get home to their families by six, too. But I occasionally did it at the expense of some people's feelings. And I think there's something to learn from that.

Amplifying the Positive

Throughout my career I've made a point to go out of my way to make people feel good. And that's an area where the voice amplification of my position would not only have a booming effect, but get broadcast far and wide with just the simplest acknowledgment. If some young soldier was doing particularly great on any particular day, I'd stop and call his or her mom or dad: "Hi, this is General Lynch. I just wanted to let you know that your daughter's doing extraordinary work here in the army; you should be really proud of her."

Other times, especially when we were overseas, I wrote letters home. I sent personal notes to family members, just thanking them for their service. Letting a wife know that her husband's service was appreciated, as was her sacrifice. I can't tell you how much a note like that is appreciated by a wife who hasn't seen her husband in months and has been left behind to tend to the household on her own. I sent notes to veterans, too, thanking them for all they had done—letting them know that their efforts would never be forgotten. I still do it. It only takes a few moments of my time, and I know those letters have an impact that lasts for years. Sometimes lifetimes.

Whether it's coming from a general, a CEO, a president, or any other type of leader, those types of notes inspire pride. They get hung up on the fridge, or maybe tacked up on the church bulletin board. Sometimes they get framed and hung up in a special place in the home, maybe passed on to someone's children after they're gone. The effect of that simple acknowledgment is powerful because it's coming from a leader—a leader who's reaching out and touching people's lives.

I sometimes get resistance to these sorts of things in the corporate world. I'll have people stand up in the middle of a presentation and flat-out ask me, "Can you do that if you're the CEO of a private business?"

The answer is, "Yes! Why not?"

"Well, *should* you do it?" they'll wonder. "Isn't that crossing some sort of line?"

My answer is, "Of course you should do it."

What is leadership about, anyway? Who is it you're leading if not your people? We're all people. There is no "us" and "them." We're all in this together. There is no line. Your impact on the lives of your people is powerful, whether you want to believe it or not. Why not indulge it in the best way possible?

Leading from a disconnected place, leading from on high, leading from afar, as if your people are just numbers or just cogs in the wheel, isn't the kind of leadership we need. What we need is engaged leadership, in every organization, in every company, and in every facet of American life. The more engaged we are in each other's lives, the stronger our organizations and, frankly, the stronger our country will be.

As I continue to do my best to walk the walk when it comes to my beliefs and principles, I find myself more and more engaged as a leader with each and every step. I'm thankful for that. I'm grateful for that. And I'm a better leader because of it.

As you read the next section of this book, I hope you'll understand why.

PART 3

ENGAGED LEADERSHIP

Do nothing out of selfish ambition or vain conceit. Rather, in humility value others above yourselves.

Philippians 2:3

If there's one subject I'm particularly motivated to share about, it's engaged leadership. I'm known for and love that phrase. It's a phrase that I hope will inspire leaders everywhere to step out of their corner offices, get down from their pedestals, and lead where it counts: among their people.

Manage by Walking Around (MBWA) isn't a new concept. If you want to know what's happening in your company, you need to get out and walk around. Talk to your people. They know what's going on, and chances are if they see you and see that you care, they'll be ready and willing to tell you all the information you need to know—and then some.

Of course, it is my belief that leading is about much more than just "managing," so engaged leadership takes that MBWA concept one giant leap further. In my view, it's not enough just to see your workers in the workplace. You need to engage them in their lives. Get to know them. Get to understand them. Let them know you care not just about their output in the office or out on the battlefield, but that you truly care about them as people. Once that's established, you'll find that your people are not only working for you, they're working *with* you.

And believe me, there is simply no stronger place a leader can lead from.

16

Leading Where It Counts

I often think about the phrase "What would Jesus do?"

Whether it's strangers on the street, people I know, members of my family, or my superiors, co-workers, and subordinates in the workplace, I always do my best to treat people with kindness, compassion, and caring.

Sarah and I have a general rule that we won't walk by anybody without addressing them, and if possible, addressing them by their first name. If we're at the grocery store or Starbucks and someone has a name tag on, we'll look at that name and address them by it: "Thank you, Mary, for your service."

On the one hand, it's just a nice thing to do. On the other? It's a shrewd thing to do. Let me explain.

In Colin Powell's latest book, *It Worked for Me*, Colin talks about the importance of addressing others by name. When he was secretary of state, he did what I do now, which is manage by walking around. Spend more time walking around and talking to people than being in your office.

One time Colin wandered down to the underground parking garage at the State Department—the first time anybody down there had ever seen a secretary of state. He just wanted to meet all of the people who worked in the building, and while he was down there he asked the parking attendants some questions. It was a very condensed parking garage—the cars parked in rows. At the end of the day, the car that was parked three cars back wouldn't be able to leave until the car in front had left. So he asked the guys, "How do you determine who gets parked in front?"

And the parking attendant answered, (and I'm paraphrasing here), "That's easy. It's the people who address us by our name, who care about us, who ask how we're doing and listen for the answer."

The people who drive in with their heads down, toss the attendants the keys without eye contact, and treat them as lesser human beings get parked in the third row—and wind up losing an hour leaving at the end of every day.

I like that story, and it makes a whole lot of sense to me because I've encountered that sort of thing in my own life. Haven't you?

Studies have shown that you can improve service by 80 percent if you address people by their first name. Why would anyone want to miss that opportunity, in work or in life? To not do that is the opposite of shrewd, not to mention the opposite of how we should be treating our fellow human beings. As a leader, addressing people in the workplace, personalizing your communication with them in the hallways, even down in the parking garage, that's just the tip of the iceberg when it comes to caring for your people.

Why should you care? When people are treated better, when people feel better, when morale is better, you get better results.

I have always said in reference to subordinates, "Take care of them and they will take care of you." As a leader it's important to "look down, not up." To focus on your subordinates. Every day your staff has a decision to make: Do they simply do their job, or do they do their job to the absolute best of their abilities? When people know that their leaders (and managers) have their best interests in mind, they will work harder. Every time.

So the question then becomes: How do I take care of my subordinates, especially in tough times?

Show 'Em That You Care

Morale is improved pretty easily with increased resources. Time off, pay raises, increased benefits, perks, you name it—the more you dole them out, the happier your workers will be. Some of the most successful companies with the highest productivity and most loyal work forces have proven that time and time again.

Morale is also improved by putting policies into place that put your subordinates and their families at the forefront. I proved this at Fort Hood when I significantly reduced the hours our soldiers were putting in and outright eliminated weekend work, but didn't see one iota of decline in our ability to accomplish missions as a military. It was proven over and over again when in the midst of those reduced hours, and the increased family time allotted for soldiers and their families, we saw improved safety and other quality-of-life factors across that installation.

But one big key to improving morale—and by default, improving productivity and getting better results from your organization as a whole—is simply increasing communication. It starts with addressing your subordinates by name. That's step one. Show them that respect. Do them that courtesy. And then, quite simply, talk to them!

"People don't care how much you know until they know how much you care." This is something Sarah taught me, and I refer to this truth often. If you demonstrate to your staff that you truly care, then they're going to be more receptive to your ideas, your thoughts, your directions. Just like the story of Colin Powell and the parking attendants, when you demonstrate that you care—like calling an individual by name and saying, "Thank you for what you're doing. How's your family?"—they treat you better. How do they treat a leader better? By doing better work, showing dedication, and stepping up when it matters.

Of course, stepping up when it matters goes both ways. Once you become a leader, or even a senior manager, there is no such thing as a casual conversation. It just doesn't exist. When you ask somebody,

"How are you doing?" and they give you an answer, they expect you to do something with it.

If you work for me and I say, "Hey, how are things going?" and you say, "I'm struggling with my finances" or "I'm struggling with my health," you're going to expect me to do something about it. As a leader you've got to truly care, truly listen to the answer, and do something. Maybe you need to give that person some more time, or help get them into counseling. Whatever it is, they're going to expect that you do something, or at the very least have someone else follow up and check in on them.

If I were just a manager I might not care as much. I might think, "As long as you're on time and you get your work done, I don't care what happens after you go home."

But I don't want to be "just" a manager. I want to be a leader. And I think it's important for you to make that distinction in your own mind.

I believe that leaders should love their subordinates the way they love their own children. I've practiced that from the time I left West Point through today. And the root of that belief goes back to the biblical message that to lead is also to serve; that in order to lead in a meaningful way, you have to have a servant's heart. To put it bluntly: You've got to care about people to be a leader.

You can't be a true leader without care, compassion, and concern.

I find myself around a lot of managers when I'm out in corporate America. They want to manage the operation, but when it's quitting time they don't want to have to worry about the people; they don't want to think about them until the next day when they come in and start work again. Management is pure business. That's all it is. It's profit and loss, trying to meet the bottom line—time cards, pay schedules. A leader has to be a good manager, of course. But I don't think being a good manager automatically makes you a leader. Certainly not a *good* leader.

So assuming you want to be a leader and that you do care about people, how do you let your people know that you care—beyond the one-on-one interactions you have with them from day to day?

You take your message to them in person.

Getting in front of your people and advocating for your beliefs and expectations is part of engaged leadership. The act of being seen, in and of itself, is powerful. And getting in front of your people to tell them how you plan to use your position as a leader to advocate for a better life for *them*? That's just plain good business. Because, and I repeat this often, when people are treated better, when people feel better, when morale is better, you get better results.

Of course, it isn't always easy to increase morale, and I found this out the hard way in my career after I left Fort Hood.

When I first arrived at the Pentagon, it was a miserable workplace environment. Almost everybody seemed to be looking down all the time. Almost everyone I encountered in that massive building seemed angry or irritable. Almost nobody made eye contact as they walked the halls. The overriding daily sentiment was, "I had a terrible commute to get here, I've got a terrible job, I have a terrible commute to get home, and it ain't gettin' any better than this!" There were any number of people who had two-hour commutes in each direction on a daily basis. No wonder everybody's basic mood was, "My life sucks."

I had five hundred people assigned to me when I first arrived, and I said, "We're just not going to continue with this misery."

I decided to implement the same sort of life-changing time-management principles I had put into place at Fort Hood. It didn't matter to me that this was a completely different environment, with a completely different sort of work force. People deserve a life. They deserve to be home with their families for dinnertime. I wanted to communicate that message to my staff, so I did something I had done with our soldiers on base all the time: I called a town hall meeting.

"Here's the deal," I said as I stood in front of all five hundred workers. "I want everybody home for dinner by six." I was naïve about Washington commutes and Washington traffic, so some people came to me afterward and said, "Well, General, here's the deal, we can leave at five like you want us to and be home at seven, or we can leave at six and be home by seven. What do you want us to do?"

Upon analysis, I realized they were right. The commute around D.C. is one of the worst anywhere in the nation, and rush hour peaks between 3 and 6 p.m. So I relented and said, "Okay, you can leave at six, but you've got to be home by seven for dinner with your families."

Even after that I got resistance. It was amazing to me. At Fort Hood, that policy was embraced with open arms. The families said, "Thank you, General! We finally have our spouses back, our husbands back, our moms and dads back." But at the Pentagon? They were so locked in to the way they'd been doing business, they didn't want to believe that this policy could improve their lives. They somehow thought that if they didn't stay later, they'd have more work to do! But I tried to apply the same mandates I applied at Fort Hood, and eventually we got some results. I held monthly town hall meetings to talk about this issue, along with lots of other issues, so my work force could see me and understand that these things truly did matter to me. To prove to them that *they* mattered to me. Still, the results were never great. I think it would take years of massive changes and follow-through to make a dent in the culture of despair at the Pentagon. But I think it's fair to say that at least some of my employees were happier as a result of my policies, and any result that yields happier employees without a decrease in productivity is a major win in my opinion.

The thing that mattered even more than the policies I put into place was the message I was trying to send. As I've said, I believe that constant communication is critical to strong leadership. You've got to talk to your work force as often as possible. And not just by email. When you type and send an email, you have no way of knowing if the person on the other end understood the email, or understood the passion and tone that you were trying to convey in that email. You just don't know—unless you talk about it. And when you're sending missives and directives to large numbers of workers, or to your entire work force at once, you have to have forums in which you talk to them in person to follow up. It gives a chance for your workers to see and hear and feel your passion for whatever message it is you're trying to send.

I put that notion into practice in a major way at Installation Management Command (IMCOM), which I ran simultaneously as I worked at the Pentagon. Now, IMCOM is 163 installations worldwide. It's 120,000 people, 118,000 of which are civilian employees. So it's about as much of a real-world an example as you can find anywhere in the military. That IMCOM commander job was headquartered in San Antonio. Splitting my time between Washington and Texas was not easy. It left me rushed most of the time, as I spoke about earlier. Regardless, I made the time to get out and talk to that work force, my people, in person.

Sarah and I visited eighty-two out of those 163 installations during the two years I was in command. We'd land. We'd get a tour. Then Sarah would go off and meet with families who had lost a loved one, families who had exceptional family members (children with medical issues), and service providers. I would spend time meeting with installation leadership, focusing on infrastructure issues, security issues, and more. And then I'd hold a town hall meeting so everyone could see me—their commanding general—standing alongside my wife, so they'd get a feel for what kind of a leader I was.

Up on those stages, I spent a lot of time advocating for work-life balance.

"You've got to be able to get your work done during the day so you can be home at nighttime" was my message, which always elicited applause. I established the 6 p.m. dinnertime rule, and it was well-received with the IMCOM work force. Again, an almost entirely civilian work force. But the message was bigger than that. It was at one of these town hall meetings in Fort Leavenworth, Kansas, where that mother and her thirty-two-year-old daughter decided to spend more time together after hearing me speak. It was only one week later that the daughter passed away. My message got through and yielded results, which in the case of that mother and daughter, was a life-altering experience. I can't tell you how many times even hard-nosed managers hear that story, get a tear in their eye, and then tell me, "I have to do something about this." If they care one iota about people, they agree that the consequence of working people too hard and too long for no reason, especially when the same results could easily be achieved during a more efficient workday, is ludicrous.

I also spent time on those stages explaining to them why things were the way they were—why certain cuts were being made, why certain decisions had been made, and what I was going to do as a leader to make their lives better while we went through some tough times as an organization.

I cannot stress to you enough just how important that was. My talks had a visible effect on the morale of the IMCOM work force. And as a result, across all 163 installations, all indicators of performance showed marked improvement during my tenure because the work force was happier, better adjusted, and felt that they were truly being cared for.

As a leader, standing up for what you believe in, and sharing that message with the people you're leading—whether one-on-one or as a massive group—makes a difference. A real difference.

Communication means everything. Especially when one of the things you believe in most is the very audience you're talking to.

— REMINDER —

LOOK DOWN, NOT UP.

"People don't care how much you know until they know how much you care."

17

Mentorship

Learning is something that should never stop. We need parents, teachers, guidance counselors, preachers, and more in our lives to help guide and teach us when we're young. I think that's obvious. And as we grow into adulthood and grow into our careers, it is my firm belief that we need something more: We need mentors.

I aggressively sought out mentors at every step of my career, whenever I had a promotion coming up. It didn't matter whether I was moving up to division commander or battalion commander or three-star general, I sought out mentors who currently held or had previously held those positions—individuals who had "been there and done that" who might be able to offer me some cogent advice and counsel. As a "mentee," I knew these individuals had learned lessons by experience that I wanted access to, so I put in the time to track them down, to get through their gatekeepers (if they had them), to make contact, to introduce myself, and to glean whatever knowledge I could from them.

I went searching for advice and counsel from some pretty well-known individuals at times, like George Casey, who had commanded the First Armored Division, and Marty Dempsey, who had also commanded the First Armored Division. You've got to aggressively seek out those types of mentors in whatever field you're in. It's not always easy to reach them, and you can't let the gatekeepers deter you. The same goes for someone who's becoming a COO or a CEO for the first time. Everyone goes into a job relatively cold, so it only makes sense to learn from people who've done it.

In almost every case, I found that those people were receptive to my seeking them out and answering the questions I wanted to ask. Some people were so busy they didn't want to take the time to talk to anybody, but in most cases I found the mentors I needed, even if they were short-term mentors.

If you want to learn about something in life, go ask an expert—someone who's living it, who's actually doing it—and 90 percent of the time those people will give you answers. People like to talk about what they do. They like to share information about what it is that they've accomplished. In general, people who are good at what they do *like* to be mentors. If you aspire to do new things in your career, go and talk to people who've already done it, see how it went, and see what the issues are.

I do not think my career would have been nearly as successful had I not done that, and I'm always surprised when people tell me they're not doing that in their own careers.

In order for organizations to perform smoothly, I believe organizational leaders need to assign mentors—to tag someone to "pick up the new guy" and show him the ropes. It doesn't necessarily have to be someone in the new guy's chain of command, either. Just someone who's been in the organization long enough, and is dependable enough, to share some expertise and get the new guy through the water. I've never understood the corporate mentality of "sink or swim." If a new guy jumps in and winds up sinking, doesn't that drag everyone else down with him? Or at the very least slow everyone down? Of course it does. Assign a mentor and that problem is solved.

Organizational mentorship needs to extend beyond the "new guys" as well. Let me share a stark example of this that we discovered in the army. Prior to 9/11, we had a mass exodus of captains from the United States Army. They were leaving in droves. The army's chief of staff at the time formed a blue ribbon panel to investigate why these captains were leaving the army, and I was a part of that panel.

Guess what one of the primary reasons was for the exodus? You guessed it: a lack of mentors.

The captains we interviewed said, "We're leaving because nobody's talking to us." They were referring to all of us senior leaders.

"Sure, we get emails from you about this and that, but nobody's taking time to counsel us. Nobody's taking any interest in our careers."

Nobody was counseling them or advising them on what they needed to do to advance their careers in the army. Nobody was talking to them about what to expect should they be promoted. Nobody was working with them to foster their careers, so they simply chose to seek careers outside of the army once they had the chance.

We asked these exiting captains, "How many of you had a mentor at any time during your time in the army?" and approximately 25 percent said they had. But when we asked the senior leaders how many of them had acted as mentors to their captains, 75 percent said they had been mentors! A big disconnect.

I think the problem lies in the definition of *mentor*. A mentor isn't just a higher-up. A mentor isn't just a supervisor or a manager. And the mentor-mentee relationship is not something idle. In the army at that time, our senior officers were not aggressively seeking out captains to mentor. But on the flip side, those captains were not aggressively looking for mentors themselves. So the relationships just never developed.

In my mind, in addition to being someone with knowledge and expertise, a mentor is somebody who is accessible, who listens, and who truly cares. And the most powerful mentor-mentee relationships are not something mandated by an organization, but are voluntary relationships between two people. Relationships based on caring.

I've had six primary mentor relationships in my life—with six guys who have a tremendous amount of wisdom to share, and who

I know I can always reach out to and say, "I've got this question." When I do that, I'm absolutely convinced that they're going to take the time to listen to me, that they're going to care, and that they're going to give the best counsel they can.

The first mentor to me in the army was Walt Ulmer, whom you may recall I met when he was commandant of cadets at West Point. He was the one who put me on the panel to investigate the cheating scandal, and whom I reported to directly in that extremely difficult time at the Academy. When he retired from III Corps at Fort Hood (the corps that I took over upon my return from the surge in Iraq), he went on to be the CEO of the Center for Creative Leadership in Greensboro, North Carolina. He took that national organization and made it into an international organization, and he continues to be actively involved in leader development. So he's still a great mentor to me, and he has lots of experience transitioning out of the army in much the same way I have. But I still have lots to learn from Walt.

The second mentor is the guy who gave me the opportunity to command two companies early in my career: the great Doc Bahnsen, who was awarded a Distinguished Service Cross and five Silver Stars in Vietnam. He's a bona fide war hero. Doc showed me what it looked like to take care of soldiers, and how to be a leader—not just in title but in actions. He's still actively involved in leadership development in his retirement in West Virginia.

Major General Tom Tait is another important mentor of mine. Tom Tait was the commanding general of Fort Knox who asked me if I wanted to transfer to armor branch, and to whom I said, "Sir, I've been trying to be an armor officer for nine years!" Tom is the man who called armor branch the moment we landed and said, "Make Lynch an armor officer or you're fired!" He carried a big stick everywhere he went. He was the epitome of a commander who was out and about all the time. He's retired now and actively involved in activities at the Virginia Military Institute.

A guy named Butch Funk is my fourth mentor. He was the corps commander when I was a battalion commander at Fort Hood. He taught me what commanders do outside of headquarters. It was impossible for me to take my battalion out for training and not be visited by Butch, no matter where we went or when. Butch Funk spent zero time in his headquarters going through long, laborious staff meetings; he spent all of his time out and about.

My fifth mentor is Fred Franks, who retired as a four-star general out of the army's Training and Doctrine Command, and commanded the VII Corps in Operations Desert Shield and Desert Storm. Fred taught me a lot about being a more senior leader, including the notion that you should never ask questions that you don't want to hear the answer to. He's also responsible for instilling that lesson about taking time to think: "Decide when to decide." In a tough situation, the first decision you make is, "When do I have to decide?" You want to give yourself as much time as possible to weigh options and get answers, but you need to know when it's time to make a decision and get on with it. That's so important. Freddy Franks taught me that.

Finally I want to mention Ben Griffin, another four-star general, who served as the commanding general, United States Army Materiel Command, before his retirement in 2008. Ben was my division commander when I was an assistant division commander (ADC), and he taught me an important lesson on experiential learning, a topic I'll discuss later. When we first met, Ben had a choice to make me either the ADC for maneuver or the ADC for support. As you know by now, I've never had much interest in being the support guy, but he intentionally chose to make me the ADC for support so I could learn about that side of division operations *before* I became a division commander myself. He made it clear that he cared about my career from the outset. He wanted me to learn, so he put me in an environment where I was uncomfortable—but I sure learned a lot. In fact, looking back on it now, I know for certain that had he not put me in charge of support, I'd have been a much less effective division commander later on. Ben's mentorship through the years has been invaluable.

Those are six people I've been blessed to call mentors over the course of my career, and I'm in routine contact with them to this day.

But it's also important to remember that mentoring is a two-way street. As you move up in your career, if people come seeking your advice, it's important to take the time to get to know them a bit and share whatever advice or knowledge you can. In some ways, that's the very definition of "engaged leadership." In order for people to have mentors, we leaders need to be mentors to others. And believe me, you'll learn from the experience, too. The process of teaching and sharing what you know is always enlightening. Ask any teacher and they'll tell you!

I've personally mentored a great number of people through the years. Even after leaving the army, today I mentor many, many folks who either worked for me in the past, work for me now, or who have sought me out for mentorship outside of their chain of command.

You're Never Too Important to Care

If you want to be an engaged leader, you've got to be a purposeful mentor—not just for the people who currently work for you, but to the people who work around you, the people who *have* worked for you, and the people who may work for you in the future in your particular area of expertise.

The first step is to open your door. In the military, just like in corporate America, the biggest problem with finding a mentor is the gatekeepers. Potential mentors aren't available or accessible, because there is a gatekeeper who gets in the way. That's why I routinely pass out my personal email and cell phone number, so that people know they can get in touch with me. Even to this day, as I'm trying to develop relationships with leaders across the business world, it's hard for *me*—Lieutenant General Rick Lynch—to get through the gatekeepers. They are paid to block access, and they do a great job of it!

So if you're the CEO of a corporation, you've got to figure out how to do this. You can't sit down with your gatekeeper and simply say, "Okay, open the gates." That's not what you want to do. You need to figure out how you can be accessible in a healthy way both for you and for those who can benefit from your mentorship. Your organization (and you) will be better for it.

Then, once you have that accessibility, you have to do the really tough thing: You have to actively listen. That's not always easy. The hardest thing I do is active listening. In general terms, I believe most of us are lousy listeners. You see it all the time as you're talking to people, when whomever you're talking to is looking over your shoulder, seeing what else they could be doing. It's hard to focus on the matter at hand and make the person who's speaking feel like they're the most important person in your world at that time.

I've spent a lot of time trying to learn how to be a better listener. It's one of my weaknesses. I've got to consciously make the effort, because my mind is racing all the time. That's the way I am. I'm always thinking about other things, thinking about what I should say, thinking about what's next on my agenda as opposed to being in the moment. But I've worked on it. And over time, I think I've learned to be pretty good at it.

Then that last piece of mentorship, the way I define it, is to truly care. To demonstrate that you're not only listening, but that you also truly care—and not just about the person's role in your organization or his or her career, but about what's best for the individual person.

Let me give you an example of what I mean.

I'm a mentor to someone who was a one-star general. When the promotion board began meeting to decide who to promote to two-star, major general, he found out he was in the running. He called me, as his mentor, and said, "As I look into the future, I'm not particularly excited about being a major general. I like what I'm doing now, but I can't see doing something that I don't like." He knew I had been a two-star general, and he wanted to pick my brain so he could make an informed decision.

To understand where he's coming from, I have to tell you a little bit about his life. Some time ago, his wife died of cancer. I was at her bedside with him when she died.

A lot of men might have been knocked down for good after something like that. In time, he wasn't. He got remarried. He's got a five-year-old son. And you can bet he doesn't want to miss any time he doesn't have to miss with that wife and son of his. He knows firsthand just how precious and unexpectedly short life can be.

When you're a general officer in the United States Army, you're busy. You're not spending as much time with your family as you'd like, even if you concentrate on it and spend quality time, as I have always tried to do. Couple that knowledge with the knowledge I have about where his priorities lie, and I'm in a pretty good position to give him advice.

He knew he could get ahold of me, he knew I would listen, and I listened hard. He asked me this question: "Do you think I should opt out of consideration for becoming a major general?"

If you've paid any attention to anything I've said in this book so far, you can probably guess my answer. I said, "Yeah, I think you should opt out. You've gone far enough. You're always going to be 'the general,' because you're going to retire as a general. But if you're going to do the right thing for yourself and for your family, you should opt out."

That was my advice.

He was going to do what he wanted to do. A mentor is not a dictator. Not even close. He asked for my advice and I gave it to him. And I did not give him advice based on what was necessarily best for the army. Being a mentor isn't the same as being a coach. I wasn't pushing him to go further in the sport, to go for the promotion, to get over the hurdle and win, win, win. That's something different.

As a mentor, I'm looking out for *him*.

If he said, "Thanks for that, but I'm going to go be a major general," and if he wound up being unhappy with that decision, I wasn't going to say, "I told you so. Why didn't you listen to me?" The decision wasn't up to me. It was up to him. And I would respect whatever he chose.

He and I have a three-decade relationship. He and I cried in each other's arms when his wife died. So I based my advice on what I thought was best for him. If he leaves the army, frankly, that's bad for the army because he's a superstar. But somebody else will step up and be a major general, and the army will go on. When I left as a three-star, I didn't leave thinking, *I let the army down.* I knew that somebody else would step up and be the four-star and do as well or better than I could have done.

I'll reiterate this point: The way I define it, a mentor isn't just someone who teaches you the ropes or pushes you to the next promotion like a coach. It's different. It's someone who can really listen and help you to figure out what's best for *you.* And you need to be both a mentor and a mentee in your career to be effective in that capacity.

Diversity is a big part of developing effective mentor-mentee relationships as well. People are different. And people who are different want to look up to people like them and aspire to be like them, whether it's a race issue, a gender issue, or something else. So if you mentor people, a lot of times you mentor people that aspire to be like you. That's the natural gravitation of the mentor-mentee relationship. But having diverse opinions and points of view in mentor-mentee relationships is a good thing.

Also, when you're the one asking for advice, it doesn't mean you have to copy what someone else did. It just gives you a chance to learn. Think of it as something that will inform your decisions, but know that you still need to make your own decisions.

That's exactly what that one-star general mentee of mine did: He took my advice, considered it thoroughly, but made the decision to stay in the army and become a two-star general. I'm not hurt by that. I'm proud of him for making the decision that was right for him. And I'm happy for the army because they get to hold on to one of their superstars.

Back when I decided to branch-transfer, one of my mentors told me not to do it. "You've already established yourself as an engineer. You're going to struggle as an armor officer." But I did it anyway. I went with my gut. And none of my mentors were thin-skinned about it. Their counsel was extraordinarily important. They let me know the risks. They made me think long and hard about following through before I did it. And when I did go ahead and do it, and

I turned that transfer into a massive success, perhaps it gave those mentors a different perspective on the matter.

Having mentors and being a mentor are two of the greatest ways to keep learning—not only while you're on the road to becoming a leader, but once you've established yourself as the type of leader that others aspire to become.

REMEMBER

BE A MENTOR.

"You must be accessible, you must listen, and you must truly care!"

18

Asking Intrusive Questions

In school we got counseling all the time to let us know how we were doing and how we could improve. Think back to your high school education: Your teachers talked to you, your guidance counselors sat you down now and then, you got report cards and most likely had parents or caretakers looking out for those report cards and doling out some level of praise or punishment each quarter or semester.

I'm here to advocate that a grown-up version of that process is important in any work environment, and it's up to leaders to make it happen.

I wasn't counseled nearly enough in my early years in the army. (Come to think of it, I wasn't counseled enough in *any* of my years in the army.) When I was, I listened intently, made adjustments to what I was doing and how I was behaving, and moved forward with confidence, knowing that I wanted to please whoever it was I was working for so I could get to the next promotion on my way to becoming a battalion commander. But I was very aware that I wanted and needed more counseling along the way.

Once I became a lieutenant and had a sizable team to manage, I made counseling a high priority and got started right away. I found that the best approach was to sit down with my subordinates on a monthly basis, look them in the eye, and say, "Here are the strengths that I've observed in the last thirty days. Here are some areas for improvement that I think we ought to work on. And here are our objectives for the next thirty days."

I carried that basic approach throughout the rest of my career, including counseling to civilian workers at Installation Management Command (IMCOM) and even now at the university level. As I got more senior and had a bigger span of control, it ended up being once a quarter instead of once a month, but it was still part of my routine.

In general, my counseling sessions took an hour. I had a blank sheet of paper with three blocks of space: Strengths, Areas for Improvement, and Objectives. The reason I phrased it "Areas for Improvement" was because if you say "Weaknesses," people take that personally. In the military, if you tell somebody you "got counseled," the first thing they asked was, "What did you do wrong?" So it's important to find ways to move counseling out of this negative connotation.

Once the basics about work were finished, I always used those counseling sessions as an opportunity to ask what I call "intrusive questions." They were human questions.

"How's the family?"

"How are your parents?"

"How's your home life?"

"Is there anything I need to know about that might be affecting your performance?"

"Is there anything going on in your family that we should be a part of?"

"Are your kids doing particularly well in school? Perhaps I could send them a note of congratulations?"

Engaged leaders ask intrusive questions. People don't care how much you know until they know how much you care. And I always found that to be a powerful time at the end of those sessions.

Don't get me wrong: I got my points across. If I wasn't satisfied with how someone was performing, in the course of the counseling they got that point. But it wasn't negative. It wasn't, "If you don't straighten up I'm gonna fire you!"

I would finesse it so that when the counseling was done, they knew their performance had to improve. But at the same time, they knew that I cared just because I was taking the time to talk to them.

As a three-star general I was counseling two-star generals and senior-level civilians—guys who had been in or around the military for thirty-five years. And I realized one day that in my thirty-five-year career, I had only been counseled like that on maybe five occasions! Only five times in thirty-five years did one of my leaders sit me down and say, "How are we doing? What can we improve on? What are our objectives for the next thirty days?" And notice the use of pronouns: "we" and "our."

It's important not to make the person you're counseling feel like you're on the attack or putting the entire burden on them. You want to make it known that you're in this together. Asking the intrusive or personal questions definitely helps smooth that over.

I've found that some leaders and managers are uncomfortable asking intrusive questions—as if somehow we're violating privacy or asking stuff that's none of our business. The thing about asking questions is that they don't necessarily have to get answered. In the course of the counseling conversation, anyone has a right to say, "That's none of your business, General." But at least they could tell that I cared, simply because I was asking. That makes it a worthwhile endeavor.

Of course, as I've mentioned before, once you're a senior leader there's no such thing as a casual conversation. If you ask the question and get the answer, there is an expectation that you're going to do something about it—otherwise you lose credibility as a leader. I saw that example in some of the poor leaders I worked under through the years, and I vowed not to follow their example.

When you open the door and ask the question, you need to be prepared for unexpected answers. As you well know, when people go home at night, there are strange things that go on behind closed doors. People have unfortunate circumstances. As hard as this is to believe, I have had two workers who, on two separate occasions, went home to find their wives had committed suicide. One of the workers has proceeded on in his life, remarried, and seems to be doing okay. The other is having a much harder time moving on. You occasionally get answers that are quite troubling, and you have to figure out how to help, what to do, and what to watch for.

In the military we get trained on suicide prevention, and you learn that sometimes you have to ask the hard question—you have to look a person right in the eye and ask, "Are you contemplating killing yourself?"

If the answer is "yes," you have to get them help. So I'm well aware of that reality, and I know how to get someone additional counseling if they need or want it. Leaders have to be prepared to take action for their subordinates' health, the same way a parent would for their children.

So you do get answers that sometimes make you say, "Man, oh man, I wish I'd never asked that question."

But you did. And now you've got it. And you've got to do something with it.

It's all part of being an engaged leader. It's all a part of loving your subordinates the way you love your own children.

Think about this: You ask your kids intrusive questions all the time.

Where'd you go last night?

Who's that friend?

What are you doing on the Internet?

You ought to be doing the same sort of thing for your subordinates. Not for the purposes of spying on them, or to dig for negative information. Rather, to connect with them, human being to human being. Get to know your employees. I also found ways to get to know my subordinates better without asking intrusive questions of them directly, yet simultaneously making them and their families feel good about their enlistment in the army. From the time I was a lieutenant until the time I retired, I called somebody's mom or dad on a daily basis.

The process would go something like this: I'd meet some young-ster, a new arrival, or someone doing a good job, and I'd ask, "Who do you love the most? Who's the most important person to you?"

I'm aware, of course, that we have a dysfunctional society because we have dysfunctional families. I apologize to my kids all the time for raising them with such a boring existence: they've got one mom, one dad, and they're stuck with us. But most people you come across have stepmoms or stepdads, stepbrothers and sisters. I tell Sarah sometimes I need a scorecard because I can't keep track of who's who! My own parents were both married and divorced, and I grew up with stepbrothers, so I knew enough to ask that question: "Who do you love the most?" Once I got that information, I'd ask for that person's phone number, then I'd call them. I did this stateside as often as I did it from a satellite phone in the desert in Iraq. If the subordinate said the person they loved the most was their mom, I'd immediately pick up the phone in their presence and dial up Mom.

"This is Lieutenant Colonel Rick Lynch, and I just want to share some good news with you." I immediately let them know it was good news, because when people get a phone call from the army, they automatically assume that it's bad news. So I'd get that out right away. And then I would say, "I'm here with your son right now, and I'm very impressed with his work. I'm glad he's a part of our team. You've trusted us with your most precious resource, your son, and I'm going to commit to you that we're going to take care of him."

You can imagine how surprised and pleased a mom or dad or sister or granddad would be to get a phone call like that. But it was also a great feeling for me as a leader to share some good news, and to let that soldier know I truly cared about him. That goes a long way, especially down the line should things ever get tough.

I would also use those phone calls to gather a little information. I would ask Mom, "Is there anything I should know about your son?"

And she would tell me every time!

149

"Did you know that my son had an anger management problem when he was in high school?"

No, I didn't know that, but thanks for the info.

"Did you know he had a drinking problem?"

"Did you know he had suicidal ideations in his first unit?"

It's amazing how moms will open up to you when they know you care about their child. Instantly, as an engaged leader, I would know more about that soldier than I might have learned any other way. And I repeat, it was not because I was trying to spy on him, but because I wanted better knowledge of that soldier. Do you think he would've come into my office and told me he has an anger management problem, a drinking problem, and suicidal thoughts? No way! But you can get to those problems through asking intrusive questions. Making phone calls home was a powerful way I did that.

This is another one of those areas that seems to bring massive resistance in the corporate world. *Why?* Why are we separating our humanity from our jobs? It doesn't make sense. We're all in this together. Do you think your employees don't have parents, siblings, and spouses? Of course they do. Do you think they don't talk about work at home? Do you think their life in the workplace doesn't affect their home life, and vice-versa? Making those phone calls gave me more information about the individuals who worked for me so I could be a better, more caring leader. It gave the people back home a good feeling, knowing that a senior leader actually cared about their loved one and wanted to share some good news with their family. Is there anyone in that equation who isn't better for the experience? No!

Look, everybody's got problems. Have you come across a human being that doesn't have a problem? They might pretend they have no problems: "Everything's great, General. Everything's great! Having a great day."

By asking intrusive questions, you find out more about your people, and as a result of that you can help them better; and as a result of that they know their leaders care; and as a result of that they improve their performance. Ipso facto.

If you take care of your subordinates, they will take care of you.

Simple.

Just make sure you're ready to actually take care of them before you get started down this road. Be prepared to follow through. If you say, "I'm going to take care of you," but you don't? Then you lose all credibility.

Take care of your people, and they will take care of you. Neglect your people, hurt your people, overlook your people, leave your people in the lurch? Buddy, beware. Because when the chips are down, there will be mutiny.

If you need a more bottom-line argument for "asking intrusive questions" of your subordinates, think about this: Things go wrong. In any organization, there will be problems. There will be obstacles. There will be mistakes. A lot of times things went wrong in outfits I commanded. But the people who fixed those things were my subordinates. I didn't fix those things—my subordinates did, without my even having to ask.

Because I had asked intrusive questions, because I showed them that I cared, their going the extra mile to overcome problems was simply a matter of fact. They would take care of it because they didn't want to let me down.

Why didn't they want to let me down? Because I hadn't let *them* down.

Imagine how smoothly just about every outfit in America would work if we all went to work with that mentality?

REMEMBER

ENGAGED LEADERSHIP IS IMPORTANT.

"Love your subordinates like you love your own children!"

151

19

Demanding, Not Demeaning

I demand that people do their job. I've always demanded that people do their job. Being a caring leader has nothing to do with being soft or being weak. And a leader has good reason to demand that people work to the best of their abilities.

I'll use my position at IMCOM as a primary example here. The mission of IMCOM is to provide our soldiers, civilians, and their families with a quality of life commensurate with the quality of their service. That's a big task. An important task. A vital task. So I was incredibly demanding of the 120,000 employees at our 163 army installations around the world, and I had every right to be.

First off, those employees were getting a paycheck. More important, they were taking care of our soldiers and their families, our nation's most precious resource. So I wouldn't tolerate substandard performance. When I talked to people in counseling sessions or otherwise, I would be very demanding.

"This is your job. We agree? My expectation is that you're going to do your job. And if you don't do your job, then we're going to talk about what actions we have to take because you didn't do your job."

I didn't yell or scream. I was never demeaning. That makes a big difference. A leader needs to make sure he or she is demanding, not demeaning. Why? Because you're the one setting the example. You're the one setting the bar—and hopefully raising the bar—for your subordinates. As a leader, and as a human being, you're not supposed to be demeaning; instead, you're supposed to follow the Golden Rule: Treat people the way you want to be treated.

My wife always put it another way when she spoke to soldiers: "Do what your mothers taught you."

The Golden Rule is about dignity and respect. You cannot stand up as a leader and say you care about your subordinates, and then fail to show them dignity and respect—no matter how angry they might make you. To do so only sends a message to your subordinates that you do not mean what you say.

In all of my time as a senior leader, you couldn't find one human being who would tell you that I raised my voice at them or cursed at them or demeaned them in public. I don't do that. That's not my style. What you will find is people who will tell you that I was hard to work for because I was demanding. And if they were not performing, I did make it known that they were not performing, and sometimes that would happen in an open forum.

The first example that jumps to mind was out on the battlefield in Iraq. I had an intelligence officer in combat who didn't always live up to my expectations. That's putting it mildly, because, oh, by the way, in combat without intelligence, people die. *People die.* So there were times in an open forum when that intelligence officer would clearly not be performing and I'd make it a point to make sure he knew that I didn't think he was doing his job. I had every right to yell at him. I had every right to curse and swear and call him all sorts of names if I wanted to. His lack of performance was costing lives. But I didn't do that. I didn't say, "What the hell are you doing?" I didn't demean him. I simply let him know where he was failing and what he needed to improve upon—with great urgency. Lives were on the line. He needed to do better.

Yelling, screaming, cursing—none of that would have made him work any harder. It only would have put him down, and in fact might have had an effect opposite of what I desired. He might have lost respect for me and then performed even more poorly than he already had. As leaders, we have to be aware of the impact of not only our words, but our demeanor and candor. It's just the right thing to do. The Bible talks about this in Colossians 3:5–12 (see appendix 2).

At Fort Hood, my demanding that folks release their soldiers in time to be home for dinner at 6 p.m., not work on weekends without my personal approval, and release them at 3 p.m. on Thursdays for family time was difficult. On many occasions I had to get "up close and personal" with leaders who couldn't understand the importance of this, or who chose to ignore it.

There was one time a private called me and asked whether enforcement of family time was a policy or a recommendation, because in his company, it wasn't being enforced. Boy, did that make me mad! Here I was, a lieutenant general, having to take the time to place a phone call to a company commander, a captain, to explain to him that he didn't have an option. He needed to follow my orders! Even then, this captain had the audacity to try to explain to me that he didn't have a family, so my order shouldn't apply. "So why do I have to go home at three on Thursdays?" he said. I just about blew my top. This was the army. In the army, you follow orders. Plain and simple. But I kept my anger in check and explained to him—relatively calmly—the importance of leading by example. I could have yelled and screamed, I had every right to yell and scream, but I didn't.

The fact is, yelling, screaming, and demeaning in any way can get you into all sorts of trouble. There was a piece in the news just recently about a leader who's been accused by his subordinates of being demeaning. They claimed that he had a pattern of cursing at them and calling them names—and it got so bad it hit the news! Talk about terrible PR. Unfortunately, these days a lot of leaders are scared to be demanding because they think they're going to be mislabeled as "demeaning." There's a line there. I've always tried to stay on the left side of that line, and so should you. But as leaders we cannot let go of our demands.

If you want to have a high-performing organization, individuals in your organization need to be high performers. That's not rocket science, right? If you've got a headquarters of a thousand people, like I did at IMCOM, and those thousand people are high-performing people, you're going to have a high-performing organization. But if you accept marginal performance or poor performance, it's going to drag everything down, and the unit itself is going to be less effective.

So I demanded adherence to standards. I demanded that people do their job, and if they didn't do their job, then I took appropriate action, which included additional counseling, moving them to a different position, or firing them.

The danger of all of that—and it's happened in the military lately—is that people who are not performing want to file false accusations about their leaders for harassment. An equal-opportunity complaint. Some marginal performers, rather than perform, will go out of their way to find (or make up) reasons why their bosses are giving them a hard time.

So I find a lot of leaders who won't be demanding because they don't want to subject themselves to that possibility. That's troubling. As we all know, there is a good portion of our population that doesn't want to perform to standards. They want to get the paycheck. They want the job. But they want to come in and do nothing all day long.

I tell people all the time, "You can choose to be part of the solution or part of the problem." And there are some people, no kidding, who *choose* to be part of the problem. They get great joy out of coming in and causing problems.

You can't let that deter you. As a leader, you've got a job to do. Just do it.

Don't lower yourself or your standards to meet the needs of the naysayers and the poor performers. Instead, go in strong and do just the opposite.

It is imperative that you establish high standards. There are people who have worked for me in the past who've said, "The problem with Lynch is that he always raises the bar higher!" Yes, I do! *How is that a problem?* Especially when it came to taking care of our soldiers and their families as we were at IMCOM. As far as I'm concerned, our performance was never good enough. We as a nation don't pay them enough.

Take a Good Look at Yourself

I think society has it wrong. I believe that the two most important groups of people are our service members, who protect our freedoms, and our educators, who guarantee our future. But as a society, we've got them at the bottom of the pecking order in terms of pay and compensation. We pay actors and athletes an enormous amount of money, but we don't pay service members and educators even what they deserve. In order to give the service members compensation, rather than give them additional pay, it was my job to give them a better quality of life. So I always raised the bar. If we accomplished a goal at IMCOM, I didn't say, "Okay, that's good enough." I'd say, "Okay, now let's raise the bar higher. Let's raise the standard. Let's take it to the next level." That's how you create a high-performing organization—to never be satisfied. Never sit on your laurels, as they say. As a result, your people have to continually try to improve. That's a *good* thing!

Of course, you've got to walk the walk in order to instill that desire for improvement in your workers, and I constantly tried to instill that desire by showing improvements in my own areas of responsibility.

I often tell my people that the most important piece of furniture in your entire house is your mirror. Every day when you look in that mirror, the reflection back has to be somebody who's making a difference, who's sacrificing himself for the greater good, who's trying to do the best he can on that particular day. I do that every morning when I'm shaving. I ask myself in the mirror: *What do I need to work on? What do I need to do to improve? How can I be better?*

Leaders need to do that every day. When you do, your subordinates will see that effort, and without saying a word they will naturally want to emulate your improvements. It's an inspiring thing.

Just always remember that to lead is also to serve. If you reflect a servant's heart, your subordinates will understand that you don't feel you're pompous because you're the leader or because you're continually raising the bar. If you're an engaged leader, they're going to realize on some level that you're their servant. That's empowering to them, and empowering to you, too. It raises your whole organization.

How do you develop that servant's heart? How do you realize that even when you're the guy in charge, your job is really to serve all of these people who work for you?

"Hey, I'm the leader. They're serving me!" That's a more typical attitude, and that's exactly wrong. The managers are the guys who say, "Okay, seeing how I'm the guy who's signing your paycheck, you're working for me." I don't think a leader takes that attitude.

Instead, a leader looks down, not up.

A leader looks at and listens to the people he's leading. He's not just looking out for himself and his cronies, or trying to serve yet another leader he's trying to please or perhaps usurp.

A leader thinks, *I care about my subordinates at all levels. It's really important to me that they have meaningful and fruitful work, and that they have opportunities to take care of their families.*

As a leader, I'm serving them to help them accomplish what they want.

To show them this, I spend a lot of time talking to my people about their personal goals. I ask, "What do you want to accomplish? As you project yourself mentally into your future, where do you want to be?"

And then my job as a leader is to help them get there. That's a servant's approach. That's important. To lead is also to serve. Jesus talked about this.

We as a nation need to advocate to people in all walks of life how important it is to be a giver, not a taker. The best way to do that is to walk the walk: To be a leader who is a giver, too. A leader who wants and needs to do the right thing for his or her subordinates. Whether it's giving them the time off they need, or monetary bonuses, or benefits that allow them to live their lives with less stress and worry, or simply allowing space for your employees to express themselves and their ideas, you need to find ways to give. You need to serve the people you're leading in order to serve the organization as a whole.

I'll repeat these two principles, because you should never forget 'em:

Leaders should be demanding, not demeaning.

And leaders should look down, not up.

— R E M E M B E R —

BE DEMANDING BUT NOT DEMEANING.

"Everyone must perform to his or her full potential."

20

Make It Personal

When I took over IMCOM, I quickly realized that the organization had taken to spending a lot of time in quadrant 3: doing reports for the sake of doing reports, going to meetings just to plan the next meeting. With massive budget cuts looming and an imperative to clean up IMCOM's act, I launched a campaign called Stamp Out Stupid, in which I solicited ideas from my staff on how we could "do less better"—how we could improve our operations, cut out redundancies, improve efficiencies, and of course maintain (and hopefully greatly improve upon) issues of work-life balance.

How did I solicit these ideas? I gave out my personal email. To everybody.

I said, "Give me your ideas."

In the first six months I got over five hundred recommendations on how we could stamp out stupid.

They weren't all great recommendations, but I would say a good 20 percent of 'em were solid. That's one hundred ideas that helped me modify how we were doing business, right from the minds of the people who were in the thick of the work and had the best knowledge of the situation. The other emails were filled with diatribes from people complaining about their lot in life, or comments like, "They're making me work too hard." But in general, I got a slew of good ideas that were then up to me to act upon.

That personalized communication—opening up a direct line to me that the work force could tap in to—did something else as well: It gave them a sense of empowerment. It gave them a voice they didn't have before. And that's powerful. Suddenly it wasn't just me dictating ideas. It was them suggesting ideas, being heard, and seeing action taken because of it.

That brings up another important point: It's important to listen to ideas from people who aren't like you. We often surround ourselves with people of similar values, similar opinions, similar backgrounds, even similar points of view. As leaders, we need to be celebrating diversity and opening ourselves up to a variety of points of view that might be different from our own. Believe it or not, you don't have all the answers! There are a lot of very smart people out there. The best thing you can do for yourself is to find them and listen to what they have to say. I accomplished some of that with this one simple program, by opening the doors to so many opinions from across the work force.

Some people thought I was crazy to give out my personal email address. "Why would you do that? You'll be inundated! You'll never see the end of it!"

I disagreed. I care about the people who work for me, and I want them to know that I care about their ideas. Sometimes the only way to hear from people in a large organization is to open up a line of communication that didn't exist before. And in a time of steep budget cuts (which I'll talk more about in part 4 of this book), I truly

REMEMBER

ALWAYS CELEBRATE DIVERSITY.

"Don't surround yourself with people like you!"

needed those ideas. I needed the employees who were on the ground, in the thick of this organization, to clue me in to the bottlenecks and road-bumps that existed in the organization's infrastructure. Handing out my personal email just made the receiving of that critical information that much faster than any other system I could think of.

You can go too far, of course. When I was the corps commander at Fort Hood, I was aggressively trying to tell the army's story. We are America's military, and after all of my work in Iraq, having served as the spokesman for the force, I knew how important it was to let the American public know what we were up to. It's all about strategic communication, so I set up a weekly televised interview on the local television stations as well as a weekly radio interview with one of the largest radio stations in the state of Texas: WACO 100. The station's range extends from Dallas to San Antonio, and every Thursday at 8 a.m. they'd allow me to get on the air for thirty minutes to talk about America's army. They called it the Fort Hood Report.

One day I got so excited about asking for input on how we could do things smarter, I gave out my personal cell phone number on the air. Now remember, this was Dallas to San Antonio! I realized about three hours into it that I'd made a significant mistake. Everybody and their brother wanted to call and tell me their views on how I should run the corps. I eventually had to change my number. Pretty stupid. When I got home, my wife reminded me that a little bit of restraint might have been in order. But my intention was good!

Constant communication is critical if you really want to improve your efficiencies. If you want to find out what they're doing out there that really makes no sense, you've got to ask your work force because they're the ones who know. (Remember: Look down, not up!) And you've got to create an environment in which they'll feel comfortable sharing their ideas.

There are still people out there who think, *If I raise my hand and say I've got a recommendation, I'll be persecuted.* No one wants to be Tom Cruise in *Jerry Maguire*, writing a brilliant memo about change and then losing your job just because you're passionate about it. And companies shouldn't be looking to let someone go just because they're passionate about wanting to make the organization better—even if they're talking about shaking the organization on its head a little bit. After all, remember this: Jerry Maguire wound up the big winner in that movie. He never should have been let go from that agency. His views were the right views. We need that kind of passion in the work force. Leaders need to recognize and listen to those voices.

That's not always easy to do, of course. There are a couple of difficult dynamics that you're working through. One is a general resistance to change. It's called institutional and organizational inertia: "This is the way it is because this is the way it's always been." You have to work hard to break through that if you want to create a dynamic and adaptable work environment.

The second dynamic is that the people of the work force feel too paranoid to raise their hand: "If I raise my hand they're gonna beat me down, so I'm just going to accept this. I know that it's wrong, but it's just the way we do business here; if I raise my hand then I'm gonna get persecuted." That's a major problem you'll have to work through if you want to be an engaged leader.

The best way to address these dynamics is to give your people a sense of pride and ownership in the organization.

In the army, I tell soldiers all the time that I'm humbled to be in their presence. Think about what we're doing now as a nation. We've been at war for eleven years. Most of the men and women who are in the army today volunteered to join the army after 9/11—*after* we went to war. They were sitting at home, watching the most recent explosion, reading about the most recent horrific act in the newspaper, and then went out and enlisted in the army. So I tell these youngsters that I'm humbled to be in their presence. They are proud to be in the army. They have a pride in our mission—defending our freedoms and our way of life.

In the corporate world it's important to try to instill that same pride in the organization. If people are proud of the organization, proud to be part of the work force, if they feel vested in the organization, they're going to be more willing to do things to try to improve productivity, efficiency, and so forth. But you, as a leader, really have to be the one to instill that sense of ownership and pride. At IMCOM, as I did this traveling road show of sorts and held town halls to talk to our people, I would always tell the story of the impact of what they're doing on the lives of soldiers and their families.

Our job was to provide soldiers, civilians, and their families with a quality of life commensurate with their quality of service. What I tried to get my staff to believe is that they were not just making a paycheck—they were making a difference in the lives of people. I'd often say: "You've got a choice in life. You can read history, or you can make history."

What I tried to do with the IMCOM staff is to make sure they knew they were *making* history. They were working hard so these soldiers could go back for multiple deployments and not break the family. They'd come home knowing their family was still well taken care of. And it worked. We did such a good job that before I left, when we polled the military spouses and asked how many of them would like their soldier-spouse to continue their career in the military, 70 percent said yes. Seventy percent! And this was after we had been at war for ten years!

Pride and communication are a powerful combination. And the personalization of communication means more than just using your words. This is definitely a case of walking the walk—where being a lifestyle evangelist is important.

As I traveled to our army installations around the world, talking about the importance of work-life balance and the importance of family, I would always travel with my wife. People would see me, and they'd see her: The video matches the audio. If I said, "My family is important," but my family wasn't with me, that would have been an indication that maybe my family wasn't so important after all. But to say my family is important when my family is there, right up in front of them, standing with me—that's lifestyle evangelism in action. That's a level of personal communication that is seen, heard, and felt by the audience, which in this case was my staff.

Empowering the work force, making sure they feel like they're part of the organization, that they have a vested interest in working hard and doing the right thing, is important. And it's important to corporate America as well. In fact, we all know there are corporations out there that are known especially for treating their employees well, giving them perks, stressing flexible schedules to encourage work-life balance, and so forth. Some of those companies are among the top companies in all of America, and you have to be in some sort of denial not to think that empowering their work force isn't one of the core reasons those companies have done well.

I consult for H-E-B, a grocery store chain in Texas, which was started in 1916 by Herman E. Butt (hence, the initials). His son Charles Butt runs the company now, and even though they're only in Texas and have a couple of stores across the border in the country of Mexico, they are the twelfth-largest privately owned company in the nation right now. Twelfth largest. They hired me as a consultant for military outreach, and I spent a lot of time with their corporate leadership talking about how they're running their operation. Here's how they make it personal: They refer to everybody in their organization as a partner. Not an employee, but a partner. And you get a sense as you walk around that these partners really feel that they're a part of the organization, and that the organization cares for them. Doesn't matter if they're a top-tier manager, a lifelong cashier, or a high-school kid snagging carts out in the parking lot, they know the company cares for them because they see it not only in bonuses and compensation, but also through education and health benefits—the kinds of things that make workers and their families both proud and secure. That's a good feeling.

They're the twelfth largest company in America, and they have grocery stores only in the state of Texas. What does that tell you? Do you think it's a coincidence? I don't. If you want to have arguments about the chicken and the egg, I will argue every time that your people come first. When you take care of your people, they will take care of your company. Every time.

It can be done. It *must* be done.

People sometimes stand up when I'm giving talks to corporate America and ask, "How does what you did in the military apply

Make It Personal

to what we're doing in corporate America today?" The answer is simple: Leadership is leadership.

They ask, "How can we personalize the experience with our work force when our HR department is telling us not to make our decisions personal?"

The human resources dynamic in corporate America is just amazing to me. There are people out there who believe that in the HR world, you can't ask your employees complicated questions or the personal "intrusive" questions I mentioned earlier like, "Tell me about your family" or "How's your dad doing?" There's a belief that there's a line that says you can't ask your staff questions outside of what they do for you day to day. I hear that all the time. Where did those lines come from? Those lines make no sense. We're all people. We're all connected. We're all in this together. And the more together we are, the better our work is going to be. It's not that difficult. But leaders have to be the ones who define where the lines are—not the HR department!

Leaders have to be involved. We have to take care of our people.

I do see improvements from the way things were in past decades, especially in some areas of manufacturing and blue-collar work. I think about my dad. My dad operated a paper cutter. That's what he did for thirty years at Champion International, eight hours a day. He pushed a green button to start the cutter, and at the end of eight hours he pushed a red button to stop the cutter, and then he went home. He didn't care about Champion International. He didn't care how the company did. He never once believed that the company really cared about him. All he knew was that he had to go for eight hours a day, and at the end of the week he'd get a paycheck. There was no personal tie to the corporation. None whatsoever.

I think things are a little different in many companies today. Especially top-tier companies.

I had a chance recently to go tour a factory at the second-largest office furniture manufacturer in the world, HON. They are located in Muscatine, Iowa. I didn't even know Muscatine, Iowa, existed! And I went up there in the middle of winter, no less. But you could

167

tell at that factory that the workers were engaged and felt like they were a part of the organization. I hope that's a reflection of our learning more, of our understanding more and caring more as the years have gone by. Our people deserve a better quality of life than my dad had, and part of improved quality of life involves having a workplace that people want to be a part of.

As I spend more time in corporate America, it just so happens that everywhere I find happy employees, connected employees, and engaged employees, I also find incredibly strong and profitable companies.

In my mind, there is no coincidence; there is a direct correlation between the two. And in every case, the engagement, the connectivity, and even the happiness started with the precedent of the personal level of attention set by leadership.

21

Accepting Responsibility

If common sense were truly common, more people would have it.

When you step back and look at a lot of the decisions I've made and actions I've taken as a leader, the average person might say, "Well, that makes sense. That was just pure common sense. Why didn't somebody do that sooner?"

The reason nobody else did it is because common sense is not that common.

If we want leaders to get things done, we have to empower them with the authority to make bold decisions, and stand by the decisions they've made—regardless of broader perceptions, prevailing winds, or office politics.

I can't remember a time in the United States military when I took a poll to determine what decision I ought to make. I saw other leaders trying to lead by consensus and figure out what the most politically digestible option might be. The way I see it, that's leading from a position of fear—fear of repercussions, fear of reprisal, fear of getting yelled at, or just plain fear of looking bad in someone else's eyes. Part of the reason for all of that fear is that we've become a society full of blamers and doubters, full of television pundits who yell and shout about what everyone did wrong when they've never actually done anything good themselves. Look at the political ads. It's striking to me how many political ads focus all of their attention on what the other guy's done wrong, and yet say nothing about what the candidate who's running is actually going to do right. That's not what leaders do. That's not what leadership looks like. Leaders take action. Leaders make the hard choices and accept the responsibility for those actions.

I think we're demoralizing our leaders and our valued workers by not supporting them when they make difficult decisions. This applies to leaders at all levels. In the army we call it "top cover," when your leaders stand by your decision. If you don't have that top cover, then every time you make a decision you'll look over your shoulder and think, *What's going to happen if I get in trouble?*

I tried to provide top cover to all of my subordinates so they knew that if they made a decision because they thought it was the right thing to do, I was going to support them in that decision. I don't see a lot of that in the corporate world. Instead, I see a lot of CYOB (Cover Your Own Behind).

Look, not everyone is going to make the right decision all the time. But if we're leading and working from a place of fear, no decisions are ever going to get made efficiently or wisely. Leaders cannot feel constrained by somebody constantly looking over their shoulder, and neither can workers. That's one reason why it's important for leaders to surround themselves with competent subordinates before they delegate. You simply can't suffer incompetence, because that sets you up to fail. If you know you've put competent subordinates in place, then you should give them the authority and freedom they need to get the job done right. You just have to be there to back them up.

The act of accepting responsibility and being responsible for your subordinates comes in many forms. If you truly care about your subordinates the way you would care for your own children, you'll accept the fact that you're responsible to look after their safety and well-being. Corporate America is pretty aware of this in the workplace when it comes to issues of safety, workers' compensation, and so forth. But I'm here to argue that leaders need to take that responsibility one step further.

Take Responsibility, or No One Will

When I returned to Fort Hood after the surge, I realized I had spent about sixteen years at that installation over the course of my career. I wasn't taking command of a place I didn't know; I knew the place pretty well—or so I thought.

Let me tell you that walking through the door as a leader gives you a whole new perspective. Even if you think you know a place, it's important to get to know your work force all over again—how they're working and living their lives. Never assume. (You know what they say about assuming!)

I've always loved being with soldiers. I like their energy. I like their enthusiasm. In the evenings I loved going into the barracks, because that's where the soldiers lived, and I continued that tradition the moment I returned to Fort Hood. I'd always take Maggie, my Labrador retriever, with me. It was amusing because some of the soldiers thought Maggie was a drug dog. They got nervous that I was running some kind of inspection, when all Maggie was trying to do was be social. She couldn't tell marijuana from a cigarette if she wanted to. Anyway, I went through that first weekend and I was shocked. The barracks, and especially the behavior in those barracks, was nothing like it was the last time I had lived on that base. First of all, the most senior person I could find in any barracks was a specialist. That's an E-4 pay grade who's been in the army just a couple of years. I couldn't find any non-commissioned officers nor any commissioned officers.

There was no leadership presence in those barracks.

Well, you can imagine what kind of trouble a bunch of young guys—many of them living away from home for the first time—might get into with no supervision. Now multiply that a few times because we're on an army base and in the middle of fighting two wars.

There was one barracks complex that made even police officers nervous. Before the police would go in there, they would put on

171

their body armor. They knew that the barracks was so rowdy that the soldiers would throw stuff at them. These are police officers at Fort Hood, Texas! So I got my corps leaders together the following Monday to talk about engaged leadership, and to encourage them to go into the barracks in the evenings.

I wanted to know how it got this way, so I asked them, "Where is everybody?"

And the recurring theme was, "General, we're just so busy. We have so much going on, we don't have time to go back into the barracks in the evening. That's not our job. We're leaders from eight to five, and after five o'clock it's somebody else's problem."

Typical manager-speak. In my opinion, that's just not true.

Here's what else I discovered: We in the army, for efficiency's sake, had decided to turn over management of the barracks to a civilian corporation. The management was intended to take care of maintenance—issuing keys and fixing things. Property maintenance, not people maintenance.

But leaders across the corps had decided, "Oh, we turned barracks over to this civilian management, so it's no longer our problem."

I explained to them that they were wrong; it *was* their problem. So the next week we got back to having staff duty officers go through the barracks routinely at night.

It didn't take much. Just the presence of leadership in those barracks turned things around. The police stopped wearing their body armor. The blotter report—a record of action and discipline reports kept by the military police—was wiped nearly clean practically overnight. Why do you think that was? Leader presence. Leader engagement. People walking through the barracks. It was an amazing thing to me. The leaders weren't cracking down or doing anything to strong-arm our soldiers into behaving better. All they did was show up.

I also spoke directly to our soldiers. I asked them, "Who do you think these barracks belong to?"

And they replied, "Well, they belong to us."

"No, they don't! Those are United States government facilities. They belong to me," I told them with no room for doubt. "You just happen to be occupying that space, so you've got to treat it like it belongs to me, not to you."

That got through to them. It didn't take long, it didn't take all that much effort, just a little engaged leadership.

Fort Hood was basically a large city. There were a lot of moving parts. I couldn't be everywhere at once, and I had to find ways to develop partnerships with people who could help our soldiers and their families in all aspects of their lives. One easy way to do that was to get to know people in leadership positions throughout the organization. Sarah and I would entertain at our home sometimes two or three nights a week. One night it would be the school superintendents. The next night it would be the police chiefs. Fort Hood was so big that there were seven different school districts, so getting to know leaders in each area was big step forward, and their getting to know me helped improve communication on a person-to-person level. I wasn't some anonymous leader dictating policy changes. I was a partner who clearly wanted their lives to go more smoothly and wanted to see this army base become the best base it could be. It's amazing what happens when everyone feels like they're a part of the same team.

I spoke earlier about the improved conditions that came in the wake of the decisions I made to send everyone home for dinner with their families at 6 p.m. and to mandate family time and weekend time off. Along with lower divorce rates, lower rates of domestic violence, and lower suicide rates, the actions I took sparked a markedly improved traffic safety record.

In the past, in the large city that Fort Hood really was, we had a record of experiencing a traffic fatality about once every three weeks. It was dismal. Whenever you drove through the gates you would see this sign marking the number of days we had gone fatality free. It never got higher than thirty.

When I took command of the corps, I took responsibility for that number. And that number climbed, day after day, to the point where we went 245 days without a fatality. A huge improvement. A noticeable improvement. An improvement that meant the world to

173

our soldiers and our families. And I attribute that directly to this focus on the family that I put into action. Families are committed and concerned for the safety of their loved ones, so if you give them the time to focus on safety issues and doing the right thing, they're going to be more involved.

There was one more piece of the puzzle that led to the improved safety record, though: I demanded that leaders be held accountable for the safety of their subordinates—not just in the workplace, but beyond the workplace.

For example, if one of our soldiers left the gate and got stopped in the civilian world with an expired license or expired insurance card, that soldier would face disciplinary action. That's a no-brainer. But that soldier wasn't the only one to get in trouble; the soldier's leader also got in trouble.

If you love your subordinates like you love your own children, you've got to worry about them the way you'd worry about your children. You wouldn't let your son or daughter get behind a wheel without having a license or proper insurance. You wouldn't let your kid get on a motorcycle that he or she hadn't been trained to operate. So why would you let your subordinates do those things?

Under my watch, leaders were doing safety checks.

Does that seem unreasonable? Corporate America is concerned about lost workdays, lost productivity, and more. So think about this: If you can take some responsibility to help make sure your workers are maintaining basic safety standards both in and out of the workplace, saving them the time and hassle and possibly dire consequences of ignoring those standards, you're going to save yourself tremendous headaches and lost productivity that can come as a result of their ignoring the basic rules.

An army base is a little different from the rest of the world, of course, and I could take additional measures to make sure our soldiers were on their best behavior day and night. For example, I put ranks on the windshields of our cars.

Before I got to Fort Hood, there was a basic understanding that there would be no markings to designate rank on the windshields of vehicles because they didn't want terrorists to know where a general or a sergeant was.

I said no way. I wasn't afraid of terrorists in Texas. I was much more afraid of our servicemen thinking there wasn't any leadership present as they moved around the base. I wanted my people to know, regardless of whether they were on- or off-post, that somebody was watching them—and that person was a leader. You could identify a leader under my watch simply by looking at their car because, on their windshield, right underneath the rear-view mirror, we put a sticker that showed their rank. If you were coming out of a restaurant and fixin' to do something stupid, like get on your motorcycle without putting on your helmet, and you glanced up and saw a windshield with a colonel's insignia? You were a lot less likely to do something stupid, because you knew you're being watched.

Then I enforced general order number one, which was basically this: "Everything you do on base you have to do off base, regardless of the state laws." This was especially important when it came to motorcycles—the vehicles that seemed to lead to a higher incident rate of traffic fatalities. I'm a motorcycle guy myself. I've ridden a Harley-Davidson for thirty years and I've never had an accident because I drive defensively. I assume that the other guy is going to do something stupid when I'm riding a motorcycle. I make that assumption. I'm properly trained, and I wear protective gear so that if something does happen I'll survive the crash. But in the state of Texas, there is no law stating that you have to wear a helmet. You could leave the base (where helmets are required), take off your helmet, crash, and die. So I said that helmets were mandatory whether or not you're on base. I had the authority to do that. So these kids knew that if they went off base and didn't have their helmet on and got stopped, they'd be in big trouble. They also knew that if they went off base and got in a wreck, it was going to be a line-of-duty "no" determination. A line-of-duty determination is whether we're going to use the resources of the United States government to cover your medical expenses. If it's line-of-duty "no," you're on your own.

Taking responsibility for their safety, and putting measures into place that would make sure they took extra responsibility for taking care of themselves, had great results. These youngsters knew they had to wear their protective gear, they had to be properly trained, and they had to be properly equipped, and the leaders knew that if something happened to their subordinate, too bad for the subordinate, but also too bad for the leader.

When I'd get all the new arrivals together every Wednesday at three o'clock—a group that would often number around five hundred because Fort Hood is so big—I'd have the leaders stand up and I'd say, "Welcome to this great place. Let me tell you what I expect of you as a leader," and I'd emphasize this leader accountability in the area of safety. If corporate America did that, there would be much less concern about lost workdays and workers' compensation—because engaged leaders need to have a role in the safety of their workers.

On a factory floor, these youngsters working at the furniture factory or the paper factory are required to wear protective eye gear and protective gloves to operate the machinery. And if they choose not to do that and they get injured, it's my feeling that it should be bad for them, but also bad for their leader—the supervisor who's supposed to be right there and who's clearly been observing the unsafe behavior without enforcing the rules. If he's observing that behavior and he tolerates it, then he's an ineffective leader and there needs to be consequences for that.

Safety is paramount, and leaders need to be held accountable. We had a couple of fatalities across IMCOM where civilian workers were doing the wrong thing around heavy equipment and got crushed. But it could have been avoided. A leader was watching the whole thing and should have been held accountable for someone not using the right jack stands or the right protective equipment or whatever it might have been. In those cases I could hold the leader accountable for what the subordinate did by docking wages, fining them, even removing them.

You can't stop all stupid behavior, of course, no matter what safety measures and consequences you put in place. We have incidents in the military of accidental discharge. In combat, we go through detailed weapon clearing procedures, so before a soldier comes back into an operating base, he's got to physically clear his weapon, and his leaders have to check it—knowing that if there's an accidental discharge on base, somebody could get hurt. Unfortunately we had a lot of problems with accidental discharges at home, because people would go home and start drinking or goofing around and they'd pull their weapon out and shoot themselves or their loved ones unintentionally. I didn't hold the leaders accountable for that. Leaders cannot be everywhere at once. Your subordinates have to take some responsibility for themselves and their actions, of course, and there are certain things you just don't have any control over. But things like driver's licenses, insurance cards, bald tires on cars, motorcycle training—the leaders working under my command *could* have control and influence in those areas. So I made sure they did.

Whenever possible, I also encouraged my leaders to go and visit our subordinates in their homes. Again, this might cross a line in the corporate world that some people see as invasion of privacy, but I just don't see it that way. We all need to get to know one another. It's important for everyone's safety and well-being that we're watching out for each another.

It is my belief that if you're a leader, you're responsible for your subordinates and their families seven days a week. I've made that my passion ever since I became a commissioned officer. When I was in charge of a platoon of thirty-five people, I made it a point to visit my thirty-five people in their homes at least once a month. Not as some sort of inspection or invasion, but just to see how the families were doing, maybe take some flowers to the wife, bring some hamburgers over and cook up dinner on the grill. For one thing, it was fun. But it also allowed me to see how they were living.

How can you care about your people if you don't know how they're living? Only 40 percent of United States military families live on military installations. So if you care about how they're doing, you need to go visit and see how they're living. If there was a time when I was in charge of too many people to go about that myself, I had our officers go and visit the soldiers at home. Most of the time it's just a friendly thing that leads to our soldiers and officers connecting on a deeper level, so they're more comfortable working with each other and communicating. It's amazing how many personal communication goals can be reached very quickly around a backyard barbecue. But there are other times when you find something unexpected and can really help turn somebody's life around before it's too late. At one point we found that one of our off-base soldiers was in such financial straits, his kids were living in a plywood extension off the side of his mobile home. This soldier was too prideful to bring those troubles into work with him. If one of us hadn't gone out there, we might never have known. And what would have happened as that financial pressure continued to build? We all know how serious financial pressure can get. It affects everything you do. It affects your life, your kids, your health (both physical and mental), and it certainly affects your work. The long and short of it is we were able to help that soldier get control of his finances, get back on his feet, and get his kids into proper shelter befitting an American soldier and his family.

In corporate America, the idea of a civilian manager knocking on a subordinate's door is really difficult to digest, I realize this. But the concept is still important. You've got to know about your people. You need to check on how they're doing, show interest in their lives. Ask the intrusive questions that get to those answers, at the very least. You can get to a lot of issues without physically going out to their house, and I'm absolutely convinced that if you do that you'll be a much more effective leader.

As a leader, I take responsibility for every single subordinate in my care. And the only way to do that is to get leadership on all levels to take that responsibility as well.

That's just common sense, isn't it?

PART 4

THE ART OF ADAPTATION

I have fought the good fight, I have finished the race, I have kept the faith.

2 Timothy 4:7

When the chips are down, when everything's on the line, when the whole team's looking to you for answers in the face of challenges bigger than anyone saw coming, will you be able to adapt and persevere? More important, have you led in a way that will allow your people to adapt and persevere along with you?

The art of adaptation comes down to much more than a simple set of rules or guidelines. It comes down to the very roots of who you are, the foundation you've built, the confidence and trust you've inspired, and your ability to truly lead your work force, team, or troops with their best interests in mind. Throughout my own life and career, I've personally adapted to new jobs, new scenarios, new bosses, new technologies, and new challenges every step of the way. I've done it with strength. I've done it with positivity, seeing opportunities in every obstacle. And I've done it by staying true to my character and beliefs. Can an entire organization adapt in similar fashion? You bet. Adapting as a leader and leading through adaptation takes much of the same fortitude and positive attitude—only there's a whole lot more on the line. This isn't just about you. This is about everything you've done, and everything your people have done. This is about success vs. failure. This is about your company, your school, your organization, your country—and whether it'll live to see another day.

Adaptation is the key to survival. And leadership is the key to adaptation.

22

Under Fire

Sometimes bad news comes in the dark of night.

It was 4:44 a.m. on the morning of May 12, 2007, when a group of al-Qaeda operatives staged a guerilla-style attack against one of my platoons in Iraq.

The army's Third Infantry Division and Task Force Marne, which comprised the 25,000 soldiers I was in charge of leading through the surge, had barely been there a month. We were engaged in heavy combat from the start, but the thing that was knocking us down time and time again, costing losses of vehicles, progress, and lives, was the scourge of IEDs.

Improvised Explosive Devices, or IEDs, were the enemy's weapon of choice. Planted on roadsides. Buried in the dirt. Silent, invisible killers. Our platoon had set up guard in a critical stretch of important road alongside the Euphrates River called Route Malibu, which the enemy had repeatedly booby-trapped with IEDs. Our enemies were so determined to take out this route (which the coalition forces needed), that they had taken to sneaking up to the craters left by previous IED explosions, planting new IEDs, and refilling the holes. We had to stop this. Thus, the reason for our platoon's presence.

We stood guard with trip wires around the perimeter, night-vision goggles utilized, and more. But the enemy was stealthier than anyone realized. They snipped the wires. They snuck up to the Humvees. They tossed percussion grenades into the darkness to disorient our team. In the chaos they shot and killed four United States soldiers and an Iraqi interpreter—and they dragged three of my men, alive, into the darkness. Kidnapped.

There hadn't been such a disturbing incident since Jessica Lynch was kidnapped back in 2003. And the thought that three of my men were being held, possibly tortured and God knows what else by these al-Qaeda thugs, left me fuming. The first thing I did was drop to my knees and ask God for help. I'm the one who says you have to love your subordinates like you love your own children, so when something happened, I took it very personally. I wouldn't have made it through without God's help.

I immediately put every resource we had into finding those men. We offered a $200,000 reward for information. We wanted our men alive, and we wanted their kidnappers—those killers—brought to justice. The pressure was immense. And despite all of our power, our equipment, and our motivation, we made little to no progress in the days that immediately followed.

On May 23, Iraqi police found the body of one of those soldiers floating in the Euphrates. With the other men still nowhere to be found, hopes were fading. Morale was down. But I refused to give up. I reaffirmed my dedication to the search at the end of that month. I assured their fellow soldiers, their commanders, and their families that they would have all the resources they needed to keep searching, even if that meant taking resources away from some of the other tasks at hand. It was the right and only thing to do, as far as I was concerned. Those were my soldiers. My children. We owed it to their families.

Meanwhile, the surge pressed on. For six straight months we would be engaged in combat operations in this complex environment of an insurgency, fighting not only the Sunni insurgents but the ideological and organizational influences of the terrorist cells of al-Qaeda, who were backed by monetary and weapons support from Iran. Our situational and operational awareness was strong thanks to the work we'd done long ago in the deserts of California to ramp up the technology to fight this kind of war. We finally had the soldiers and resources on the ground to accomplish what we needed to accomplish, but the ups and downs of that sort of daily combat are enough to tax even the most resilient person's strength and will.

No sooner would we have good news than it would be pushed aside by something terrible. There was one day that June when two of my men used their keen eye and good instincts to stop a suicide bomber who was ambling toward one of our outposts in an innocent-looking farming truck—filled with 14,000 pounds of explosives. That intervention deserved celebrating. The American public needed to hear of that sort of bravery and action on the part of our soldiers. Yet on that very same day, another suicide bomber detonated his vehicle on a bridge we used to bring supplies up from Kuwait, killing three of my men and wounding six others in the process. The celebration quickly turned to tears, prayers, and damaging headlines.

As the months passed, the scourge of IEDs grew more frequent and severe. Roadside bombs were ripping apart our convoys and killing our men. We went out on foot looking for the insurgents who were planting these things, sometimes moving door-to-door. Routine patrols in supposedly secure areas would suddenly erupt. Men fell. The enemy's forces grew smaller with each step of our progress, but they also grew smarter. They would set up obvious IED-looking devices, forcing our vehicles to steer around them, only to hit a true IED buried down the other path of the fork in the road. On August 11, 2007, a sniper opened fire on one of our platoons along the West Bank of the Tigris River. One of the men was wounded and evacuated as the rest of the platoon rushed to the building where the sniper was hiding. Turns out the sniper was only a ruse. As the soldiers busted in, spreading through the house with weapons ready, searching room-to-room, a huge explosion ripped through the building, collapsing walls and burning some of those men alive. The entire house had been turned into one massive IED.

I lost five soldiers in a single moment.

It was the worst one-day casualty count since the surge began.

Again, I took it personally. I fell to my knees. I asked God for help.

We were making progress, but at what cost?

The Triangle of Death was living up to its name. The slaughter we witnessed, not only to coalition forces but to the Iraqi civilian population because of this insurgency, was unbearable. For six months we endured, we pushed on, we won, we suffered setbacks, we charged ahead through the intensity of battle in 110-degree heat, and pressed against the relentlessness of the insurgency not knowing where the enemy might rear its ugly head, where it may have left its hungry weapons buried just beneath the sand or just behind an unopened door.

There had to be a better way. There had to be hidden opportunities in the midst of all this hardship.

We had the "means"—our resources during the surge were immense. We could see the "ends"—the rebuilding of Iraq as a free democracy. What we needed to find was a different way to get there.

Leaders see opportunities, not obstacles, right?

As the months went on, I saw an opportunity in the unlikeliest place of all. I saw opportunity in the eyes of my enemy.

Just as I would never lead a business sitting in some corner office, I didn't lead from the safety of a hidden bunker somewhere in Iraq. I followed the basic tenets of Manage by Walking Around. I treated my role as commander in this war the same way I treated any other leadership position: as an engaged leader. That not only meant I engaged with our soldiers and officers—getting to know them, throwing a ball around with them when we could find moments to relax, picking up a satellite phone and calling their mom or dad from the field just to say hello and to let them know that their loved one was safe—it also meant that I spent time with the people we were fighting for.

The more time I spent with the Iraqi people, the more I enjoyed being around them. What I realized is they were just like us: They wanted freedom from fear, they wanted to be able to send their kids to school, they wanted a functioning government, they wanted to be able to provide for their families. Just like us. And they're educated. If Saddam Hussein did anything right, he invested in the education of the Iraqi people. Why he chose to do that, I don't know, but he did. The more I hung around these Sunnis, the more I realized that they could be a part of the solution instead of part of the problem.

Back when I was first negotiating with the Sunni insurgents in 2005 and 2006, there were multiple occasions where I sat down across the table from fifteen or sixteen of these guys, all of them armed, and they blatantly told me, "We hate you." I was able to calm things down a bit in those days just by sticking to my principles and talking to them as people; trying to diffuse the hatred by letting them know our true purpose. Letting them know that we weren't there to stay, that we wanted to help them by helping all of Iraq become peaceful and free of the oppression they had faced for so long. I was alone in those negotiations, except for an interpreter, and yet my presence represented all of America and the entire coalition force. Any one of them could have pulled a gun and blown me away just for the power trip of it, from the sheer anger they felt—especially at that point in the war when tensions between the Shia and Sunni populations were about as high as they could get. But by talking to them like the human beings they are, by looking them in the eye, by taking responsibility for what we had done and were doing, and being honest with them about our intentions, I was able to break through.

In fact, it was at those negotiating tables where I learned an incredibly valuable bit of information about the Sunni insurgents. "We hate you," they said. "But we hate al-Qaeda worse, and we hate the Persians (that's what they called the Iranians) even more." So in terms of a hierarchy of hatred, we were number three. That seemed like an opportunity to me, and eventually, as I proved in action, it was.

Even as we were engaged in combat throughout 2007, I looked around and realized that these Sunnis were no longer a united front entrenched against us. Something had changed. The majority of these people on any given day were fence sitters. On any given day they were waking up and making the decision, "Am I going to attack the coalition or not?"

Do Something Different

The tide had slowly turned against al-Qaeda in a big way, because in their desperation to hold on to what little power they had, they had turned to brutal tactics to get their way. Terrible, barbaric, terrorist tactics like slaughtering children and parading the bodies in front of their mothers. Not exactly the kind of behavior that puts you in the good graces of the population you supposedly want on your side. It was supposed to be a show of strength, instilling fear in the Sunni population so they would join al-Qaeda in the fight against the Americans. The problem is, leading by fear always fails in the end. It never lasts. Eventually, the population that's been fearful will rise up against you. I knew that. I saw that happening. And I decided to try something new.

Turns out, a lot of that daily "should I attack the coalition or not" decision was purely financial. After asking around, I realized that if a Sunni planted an IED, the insurgency would pay him two hundred dollars! The only reason the Sunnis would do that is because they had no other source of income and they had to find a way to provide for their families. And, oh, by the way, they didn't like the fact that we were there. We were occupiers. People think we were there as liberators, and that's true. But after about a week, no matter what your original intentions were, you're viewed as occupiers. Think about it: If you had somebody bouncing around your town in tanks and Bradleys, you'd feel the same way. I could understand their reasoning.

What I realized we had to do was take these potential obstacles, these fence sitters that were planting IEDs, and turn them into opportunities. What I tried to figure out was how to subsidize them so they wouldn't choose to shoot at us or plant bombs.

I had this asset called the Commanders Emergency Resources Program, the CERP program, which gave me a relatively unencumbered chunk of money to do whatever needed to be done on the ground to help our efforts. It could have been used for building *things*. Instead, I used it to build a *movement*: the Concerned Local Citizens program.

Basically, we went around and asked the Sunnis to join in our efforts to stop the violence, and we paid these "volunteers" eight dollars a day for their efforts. That was a pretty significant chunk of change, to both them and to us. Especially as dozens, and eventually hundreds, of Sunnis started to volunteer for the program. But it was certainly money well spent. It worked. As a result of that eight dollars a day, these Sunnis had a source of income, which meant they didn't have to plant the IEDs anymore. As a result of the removal of that financial stress in their lives, they were less likely to be hostile toward the coalition forces. They stayed on the right side of the fence.

By January of 2008, this program blossomed into what became known as the Sons of Iraq program. Once these Sunni volunteers stayed on the right side of the fence, they started to get interested in securing themselves rather than relying on us to provide all the security for their towns. Every day I'd spend all day walking the streets of Iraq, meeting with leaders in the local areas who had been empowered by the Sons of Iraq program. They were the first to tell us about insurgents. They would tell us, "That guy doesn't belong here. We don't know where he's from," or "Even though this guy's my cousin, he tends to do some bad things." Heck, there was one old man who started personally guarding who came into or out of his town—sitting at his self-created road block with nothing but a knife in his hand.

It didn't take long before the effects were felt all over the region. By the spring of 2008, we had 25,000 Iraqis enrolled in the Sons of Iraq program. The number of IED attacks fell significantly, almost by default. And that changed everything.

It changed the course of the war.

This all sounds logical and good and reasoned now, with 20/20 hindsight, but I've got to tell you: Turning this obstacle into an opportunity was one of the scariest things we could've done. It couldn't have been riskier. Lots of these "volunteers" had American blood on their hands. In the town of Jurf as Sakhr (pronounced "Jervi-sucker"), there was a guy leading the insurgency who was trying to kill me as I was trying to kill him. Suddenly, he decides he wants to become part of the Sons of Iraq program. So there I was, giving this man—who was an insurgent not twenty-four hours earlier—a hug on the streets of Jurf as Sakhr! He was going to become my friend, not my enemy, under this program.

Talk about risky business! These guys were wearing those loose, traditional one-piece garments, so you had no idea if they were armed as you went to shake their hands. They knew we were armed, obviously, but talk about calculated risk.

How did I know we could pull this off?

First of all, I had faith on my side. I prayed every day, and I knew we were doing the right thing. That's powerful. "What, then, shall we say in response to these things? If God is for us, who can be against us?" (Romans 8:31).

Second, I took this thing one step at a time. I was pragmatic. I didn't do this in one big sweeping move. It was locality by locality, over the course of many months. You could just get a sense from talking to the people when they'd reached that point where they'd had enough. It went all the way back to talking to the Sunni insurgents in 2006, when they told me, "We hate you. But we hate al-Qaeda worse, and we hate the Persians even more." I saw that hierarchy of hatred as an opportunity then, and here it was a year and a half later as an opportunity realized and a turning point in the war.

Of course, the biggest theme here is really just that we tried something new. As a leader you can't be afraid to try new things. The definition of insanity is to do the same thing over and over again and expect a different outcome. In this particular case, in Iraq, we were just trying something new—with a large amount of calculated risk. We were extending partnership and trust to perceived friends who could have turned out to be enemies with access to stab us in the back. But we understood the risk, built in safeguards, and found success. I had five brigade-level commanders that worked for me across the battle space. We would sit down with a cigar and say, "Where are we at? Are we ready?"

There were sixty-two patrol bases, and the young captains and soldiers who ran those bases knew the Iraqi people nearby each base. If you had those lines of communication open with them, you could get a good sense of what was happening and how ready those people were to stop being our enemy and start being a part of the solution.

But make no mistake: The call had to be made at my level because of the risk involved. If a young captain said, "Now's the time," and it wasn't the time, and he lost soldiers, his head was on the chopping block. So I had to give them that top cover I've spoken about. I had to take the responsibility for saying, "Now's the time."

I had to take that responsibility because I knew we had to try this.

I'll say it again: If something's not working, try something different.

Sure it was a big risk. On any given day I could have lost a whole company of people. They could've easily walked into an ambush. People got aggravated with me because I got to the point where I would be on the streets, in the markets, and in the houses, and I'd actually remove my body armor and my helmet. I was trying to have this relationship with the Sunni people, and when you're looking at them through ballistic sunglasses and you've got your helmet and your body armor on, it's not exactly conducive to productive conversation. They're out there in their traditional garb and you're in body armor? It just didn't work. I had to walk among them the same way I would walk among the troops back home or in the barracks at Fort Hood.

Of course, there were some cultural issues to overcome, too. For instance, the Iraqi people do communal meals. And as Americans who were now working with the Sunnis rather than against them, we all experienced "goat grabs." That's when they'll kill a goat, roast it, put it on a big bed of rice, and put it on a table. Then everybody just reaches in and grabs their goat meat. This guy you're now working with will reach in with his hand—no plastic gloves, but bare hands (and you don't know where those hands have been)—and grab some of that goat and hand it to you. If you didn't take it and eat it, they were offended. These are the same guys we were trying to kill the day before. Now I'm literally eating out of their hands! So at any point it could have become a disaster.

All of it was a calculated risk, and it really was "adapt or die." We had to change. We had to adapt. We had to find new opportunities. And we had to do it despite lingering feelings of hatred that existed on both sides.

Despite the resources I had thrown into the search, nearly a year had gone by since that 4:44 a.m. platoon attack when three of my men were dragged off into the darkness—and two of them were still unaccounted for. No amount of progress or reconciliation could alleviate that horror. The mother of one of those missing men slept with a cell phone under her pillow every night just in case someone called with any news. I was aware of that the whole time. The horrors of war, and the horror of a mother not having answers about the whereabouts of her boy for that long, haunted me.

May of 2007 is when that platoon was ambushed. In August of that year, the house-born IED took out five of my men in one fell swoop. Now here we were four months later, walking into Iraqi houses every day under this Sons of Iraq program. If we relaxed our guard, that sort of disaster could have hit us all over again. But we had to do it. We had to shift the equation. We did. And it worked. It changed the course of the war in Iraq, and it was time for yet another adaptation.

Almost overnight, I had to shift gears from combat operations to capacity building.

23

Rebuilding

The Sons of Iraq program brought some assurances of peace, but we needed one more big round of force to lay it to rest. On January 10, under my command, we dropped 47,000 pounds of bombs on military targets south of Baghdad. The strikes were remarkably effective, and no civilian casualties were reported whatsoever. Then on January 20, ten days later, just in case anyone was thinking we were through, we did it again: 34,500 pounds dropped on forty known enemy targets—most of them in a matter of minutes. We were through fooling around, and we wanted the enemy to know it.

Backed by the Sunnis in the Sons of Iraq program who wanted to stem the violence themselves, and our soldiers on the ground who never let up despite so many months of intense fighting and suffering the scourge of IEDs, the plan worked.

The tide of violence turned. And now it was time to get to work in a whole new way: rebuilding Iraq's economic, governmental, and social capacity. The Sons of Iraq program wasn't enough to sustain a healthy economy. Plus, we were spending nearly $10 million a month to employ those Sunnis and keep them on our side of the fence. That wasn't sustainable. That wasn't our job beyond the short-term fix it was meant to be. The Iraqis needed to get their country and economy back, and to start making a good life for themselves.

So I had to change my focus.

As a leader, I had to ask myself: *How am I going to get the economy up? How am I going to get the government established? How am I going to get the road networks working? How am I going to get the clinics built, the schools going?*

Frankly, those are skill sets I didn't have. No one on my staff had those skill sets, either. We're the army. We weren't trained on capacity building—but that was the situation we were in.

Look down, not up. I lived by that principal. It was no different in Iraq. When looking for answers, I went to the people. I learned that the area we referred to as the Triangle of Death was teeming with life before the war started. There were a thousand fish farms and probably as many chicken farms located in that one region south of Baghdad. If we wanted to give the Iraqi people what they needed, we needed to bring those livelihoods back.

So as we headed into the spring of 2008, this two-star general who'd spent most of his adult life living in Texas had to become an expert chicken and fish farmer.

We had to figure out how to help the Iraqi people take these baby fish, these fingerlings, to their fish farms, grow them to some level of vibrancy, and then transport them to market in 110-degree heat.

This is what we, a heavy combat division of the army, had to do in order to start to win this war—in order to continue the turn of the tide that would eventually get our soldiers out of there in 2011. I tapped my soldiers for whatever expertise they might have, I solicited ideas, and in putting our heads together we actually designed and built refrigerated trucks to transport fish to market. We figured out how to put the right facilities and infrastructure together so the fish could grow in their local farms and get sold and wind up on dinner tables.

In the chicken farming business, we sent a team to Holland to buy 50,000 fertilized eggs. We brought these eggs down into the battle space and set them up in incubators—a giant version of the little cage with a light bulb you might set up in a second-grade classroom. I learned more about growing chickens and growing fish than I ever wanted to know or thought I'd need to know, but that was what we needed to do.

The essence of an Iraqi is a sense of identity within the family. They're people of honor—and if we could figure out how to help them with their livelihood so they could take care of the family, they wouldn't need to shoot at us or shoot at each other any longer.

That's how you turn the tide in a war-strewn country hit by insurgency: by building capacity.

I realize it's funny to picture this hard-nosed American general becoming an expert poultry farmer and fish farmer. It's probably difficult to think of me touring a truck factory that we got back on its feet for manufacturing after all those months spent trying to kill the very people who might be working in that factory.

But adaptation is the key to survival. It's the key to winning. And I hope you can take some lessons from that no matter what kind of organization it is you're trying to lead. If I could repurpose my team from killing people to poultry farming and fish farming overnight, you can certainly adapt your work force to an ever-changing marketplace.

We could have maintained the status quo with the Iraqis, continued to kill them, continued to persecute 'em, continued to walk the streets of Iraq with our weapons ready—but where would that have gotten us? We had to adapt. We had to say, "No. It's time to stop doing what we've been doing. It's time." It was one region, one town at a time. But even so, it was time.

I was the one to make that call and to take that risk for my men because I knew it had to be done.

Incrementally, the Third Infantry Division and Task Force Marne began building police stations, laying water pipes, and bringing radio stations back online, in addition to reviving the fish and poultry farms. And by June, our mission was complete. There was still plenty of building to do, and there were still al-Qaeda forces to be dealt with here and there, but those tasks would be passed along to new divisions, under new leadership.

If there was a deep regret among my men, one pain that was still pulling at my heart, it was that we hadn't located those two soldiers who were still missing. We had good reason to believe they had been killed. But the fact that we hadn't found them, hadn't been able to give their parents or any of us that closure, was tough. Fortunately we got some fresh leads before we left, and by July the bodies of both of those soldiers were found. Their remains were flown back to the United States, and their parents were able to finally let go of the aching hope and painful wondering that kept them awake for so many nights. They were finally able to grieve.

I was able to grieve, too.

In the course of those fifteen months in Iraq, we lost 153 of my men and women. That's 153 sons and daughters who lost their lives based on where I put them on the battlefield—because I took responsibility for the actions of every leader and every soldier under my command. I carried laminated pictures of each of those soldiers with me wherever I went in Iraq. And I carried those pictures home with me. I placed them on my desk where I could see them each and every day as a reminder of what we had done, what we had accomplished, and the sacrifices it took for us to complete our mission. And I sought solace in Scripture, especially John 15:13: "Greater love has no one than this: to lay down one's life for one's friends."

Those laminated pictures were a reminder of just how important it was for me to make decisions as a leader knowing that every decision I made affected the life of someone under my command. In Iraq my decisions affected lives in the gravest manner possible. Back home? Well, however we affect the lives of our subordinates is just as important, isn't it? After all, we need to love our subordinates as we love our own children. I will never let go of that belief. Ever.

The army gave me my third star when I returned home from the surge. They put me in command of Fort Hood. And I knew I would do everything I could in that position to help our soldiers and their families live the best lives they could.

That was my job. That was my new mission. Fighting in Iraq, and winning—through all of the sacrifices and the lives that were taken—inspired me to want to do more. As a leader. As a husband. As a father. As a servant of God. After all, I had been gone fifteen months. I had missed a lot. I had missed two of Sarah's birthdays. I had a lot of time to make up. And as the leader of Fort Hood, I had a lot of people to look after.

I would do whatever it took to adapt to that new role, and to see to it that the people under my command were given the tools they needed to adapt to the challenges we would all be facing together moving forward. And I would do it without sacrificing my family. I would do it while enriching my life and the lives of those around me.

I came back from Iraq fired up to continue the mission of leadership I had embarked on decades ago. Only now I had all of the tools and experience to get the job done.

24

Building Resiliency

Charles Darwin said, "It is not the strongest of the species that survives, nor the most intelligent that survives. It is the one that is most adaptable to change."

I think that premise applies equally to people—in the work force, in school, in government, in sports, and especially in life. I also think that premise applies to corporations and organizations of all stripes. It's not the strongest corporations that survive. It's not the most intelligent organizations that make it. It is the corporations and organizations that are most adaptable to change.

So as a leader, you have to ask yourself: "Are my troops the strongest of the species? Are my subordinates the most adaptable to change of any subordinates out there? Is my staff able to weather the storm of competition and rapid technological change? Or are my competitors breeding a work force that's going to adapt faster, stronger, and more capably while simply leaving us out here to die?"

Then you have to ask yourself, "How do I develop subordinates that are the most adaptable to change? How do I develop a team that's capable of surviving, well, just about anything?"

Chances are if you've made it this far, if you've become a leader, if you've weathered the changes and obstacles in your own life with aplomb, you're probably what I would call a resilient person. And that's a good thing because that's what you're going to need your people to be, too.

The key to adapting to change is resiliency.

Webster's has two closely related definitions for *resiliency*. The first is "capable of withstanding shock without permanent deformation or rupture," and the second is "tending to recover from or adjust easily to misfortune or change."

Many strong examples of resilient individuals can be found in the army. Think about it: Not every soldier that deploys to combat operations comes back devastated. Many of them come back enriched.

I am one of those people.

I fought in Desert Shield and Desert Storm, spent a year in Kosovo, had two other deployments to Iraq, and then had a third period of time when I was in and out of Iraq from Naples, Italy, as part of my NATO command. When I went into combat, I saw some horrible things. I felt life-and-death pressures unlike anything I ever imagined I could survive. Yet when I came back from combat? I wasn't devastated. I was enriched! I had been challenged. I had been forced to work through difficulties, and I found that through all of that, I had grown in wisdom, strength, and fortitude. Those experiences, as difficult as they were, shaped me into a better leader. I didn't wither under the pressure. I didn't fade. I got stronger. I got smarter.

That is the essence of resiliency.

The question is whether resiliency is something inherent in certain individuals, or something that can be fostered and instilled in individuals. I believe it's both. There are some people who are born capable of weathering almost any storm. It's just in their DNA. But I've also witnessed firsthand and been a part and parcel to what we've done in the army to help build resiliency in our soldiers.

We need resilient soldiers and officers up and down the entire chain of command in the army. We know that. We want that. We fight for that. So as an army, we studied what makes a person resilient, and we found there are five key components: spiritual fitness, physical fitness, emotional fitness, societal fitness, and familial fitness.

Spiritual Fitness

Spiritual fitness is not about any particular religion. It's about acknowledging some greater power that will help you through difficult times, and that you can rely on for strength. At Fort Hood, Texas, we built a resiliency campus. I took the chapel that Sarah and I were married in and turned it into a "spiritual fitness center." Where a chapel is a place of worship, this center was a place of growth. It wasn't tied to any denomination. All were welcome. It was a place intended for folks grappling with problems to go and seek help from the higher power they believed in. It was full of literature, music, refreshments—everything welcoming and inviting. What I was trying to do was give these youngsters in the army a place to go in the middle of the night if they needed a source of strength, to be able to get that source of strength.

We'd also use this facility to gather our soldiers and share stories. I told them the story of what happened the day our platoon was attacked and three soldiers were dragged away—and how I dropped to my knees and prayed for guidance. I told them the story of the house-born IED that took five of my men, and how we worked through that—how spiritual fitness gave me the strength to keep going. I told them how I prayed for strength, courage, and wisdom every morning, and how I say the prayer of Jabez every morning, too.

For those who don't know, the prayer of Jabez is in the book of First Chronicles. The prayer is dropped in among a long genealogy that is virtually unreadable. However, the prayer itself is a hidden gem. It says, "Jabez cried out to the God of Israel, 'Oh, that you would bless me and enlarge my territory! Let your hand be with me, and keep me from harm so that I will be free from pain.' And God granted his request" (1 Chronicles 4:10).

Considering the experiences I've had down through the years, evidently God is in the business of enlarging territory. I sometimes joke that I need to stop saying this prayer, because God just keeps on granting me bigger and bigger responsibilities as a leader!

But jokes and light conversation aside, the thing I really like about that prayer is the part about God's hand being with me and keeping me from harm. And the last line is the key: "God granted his request." That's the key to spiritual fitness right there. If you believe that, if you believe that there is some higher power that will always be there for you and will keep you from harm, then you're free. Free to live. Free to move through whatever trouble you're facing. Free to face down life's fears and obstacles, from the day-to-day struggles to life-or-death challenges as big and scary as the ones I faced in Kuwait or Iraq.

Regardless of whether it's the prayer of Jabez or some other meaningful prayer, I believe prayer is part of a healthy spiritual fitness regimen. I also believe prayer can yield some pretty amazing results.

In addition to the policies I put in place at Fort Hood, I attribute much of the improved safety record we developed under my command to the power of prayer. Routinely at dinners, functions, and banquets, we paused to ask God to be with our soldiers and our families. I believe he answered that prayer. (Truth be told, I believe God answers all prayers—even if sometimes His answer is no.)

That belief is powerful. Taking a few moments to put spirituality into practice is powerful. Reading the Bible is powerful. The combination of all of that gives me peace. But it also helps me as a leader and as a human being to share that peace with others.

There were several occasions when one of my soldiers was hurt in training, and when I visited them in the hospital I'd pray to God for healing. There were many times when God granted that request, and with the help of our great medical professionals, we would see soldiers recover "miraculously." When I was a battalion commander at Fort Hood, Sarah and I, along with our chaplain, went to inform a young army wife that her husband had been killed in a vehicle rollover. When she met us at the door, she was holding her baby in her arms. And she collapsed when she heard the news. Luckily, we caught the child before she hit the ground. We prayed to God for strength, courage, and wisdom to get us through that. We reached out to her parents, who were on a cruise when it happened, and miraculously they made it to their daughter's side by nightfall.

It's stories like these that I'd share with our soldiers, to make them ask themselves what it is they believe in. Do they believe in a higher power? How do they stay in touch with that higher power? Are they spiritually fit and prepared to deal with crisis and loss in their lives—because like it or not, we're all going to face heartache and pain at some point. I know that I couldn't have made it through my time in Iraq, or just about any of the difficulties I've faced in life, without my belief in God and the devoted attention I've paid to my own spiritual fitness. So I used that space to talk about it—to talk about how I set my priorities in life, putting God first, family second, and career third. Giving your work force the time and place to worship as they see fit truly matters. People need belief in something they can hold on to when everything seems to be falling apart. It's important for leaders to provide an environment that allows that to happen—and then it's up to each individual to find those answers for him- or herself.

Physical Fitness

I think it's fairly obvious why physical fitness is important in the army. In combat, in 120-degree heat, wearing seventy pounds of body armor while people are shooting at you, you've got to be physically fit. But physical fitness is about much more than muscles, so I made sure my forces had what they needed in order to train their bodies to handle the pressure. I took one of the many gymnasiums at Fort Hood and turned it into a broad-spectrum physical fitness resiliency center. We focused on CrossFit training, yoga, meditation, Pilates, even aromatherapy to help folks control their nervous systems and learn to stay calm under pressure. We encouraged everyone to focus on all aspects of their physical well-being.

There's a book I like called *Younger Next Year*, and it stresses the importance of constant movement. Don't be sedentary. I've talked about incorporating two hours of physical fitness training into my daily routines, even in the heat of combat in Iraq, and how I insisted my subordinates follow the same routine. If we could do that in the desert while taking fire, you can do it where you live and work. There is simply no excuse for not getting the exercise and physical fitness training you need. As a leader, you can find ways to encourage your subordinates to get fit and stay fit. Build a gym at your headquarters. Can't build a gym? Start a lunchtime running program, an on-site yoga class, or make a deal with a local gym to drum up business by offering a discount for your employees. If your staff is physically fit, they will be more resilient—in their lives as well as their workplace. It literally takes strength, as the old song goes, to pick yourself up, dust yourself off, and start all over again.

Emotional Fitness

The third component of resiliency is emotional fitness.

The book *Emotional Intelligence* talks about having an EQ, just like we have an IQ. Your people need to be emotionally stable in order to face pressure and change when necessary. As a leader, you can help them by creating work environments that support emotional stability, offering counseling services through your health plan or some other arrangement, providing support services or referral services when necessary, and simply by treating your subordinates as the human beings they are.

A lot of this comes back to treating your subordinates the way you would treat your own children, doesn't it? You want—no, need—your children to be emotionally healthy and fit, the same way you need them to be physically fit and healthy.

Societal Fitness

A fourth component is societal fitness. It's important that your team members have commitments to their community, so that the community is there for them and they are there for their community. It's important that your team members answer this question well: "Is it bigger than just you?" Looking outside yourself—seeing the big picture—is an essential part of life. Encouraging and rewarding your employees for volunteer work, supporting community outreach from within your organization, and making sure that your teammates are engaged in philanthropic efforts on a local level and that your community engages on a personal level with your team—all of it can help create those powerful connections that make your people feel like the community has their back.

Familial Fitness

The final component of resiliency is familial fitness.

This one came easy to me. Putting family as a priority, making sure my workers and soldiers got home for dinner and spent nights and weekends with the people they love—that's key. Your relationship with your immediate family—no matter who it is you call "family"— is a key to happiness, stability, and strength.

A subset of the family fitness component is finances: Are you established financially? We would ask soldiers, "Before and after you deploy and come back, will you be financially fit? Do you have financial stability?"

If the answer was no, we'd work with them. Courses in budgeting, accounting, saving for retirement, and more are easy things for most leaders to set up for their people. Making sure salaries are in line with cost-of-living, and benefits are covering important pieces from medical insurance to tuition reimbursements to emergency funds when possible, can give your subordinates and their families a peace of mind that will better allow them to focus on the tasks at hand when the chips are down.

Again, most of this falls in line pretty easily when you love your subordinates as you would love your own children. You wouldn't want to see any of these components missing in people you truly care about, and the steps required to offer guidance and assistance in these areas are not difficult to take. If you truly care, you can indeed set a structure in place in corporate America and elsewhere to build resilient employees—so that when confronted with difficult times, they will come out of them enriched, not devastated.

Go ahead and let your managers complain all they want about the costs of these things. As leaders, we have to stand up and let it be known that the cost of not taking care of our people is much greater. The cost of not building a resilient work force could well mean that your company will not survive as your competition and the world around you continues to evolve. Plain and simple.

After all, Darwin's lessons aren't the only the place you'll find words about the power of resiliency and adaptation. The Bible has something to say about the subject, too: "Not only so, but we also glory in our sufferings, because we know that suffering produces perseverance; perseverance, character; and character, hope" (Romans 5:3–4).

Look at the five components of resiliency that we uncovered in our research in the army, then think about how they apply to your own organization and what you can do to foster the growth of each of those areas in your subordinates. The payoff will be immense.

25

Experiential Learning

In looking back at my own career, and almost any army career, I think there's another clear key to building resilient, adaptable soldiers: giving them plenty of experiential learning opportunities.

Experiential learning is just what it sounds like: Learning from experience.

In general terms, a member of the United States Army has opportunities to learn from institutional learning, organizational learning, and self-learning. That's generally the way it works in corporate America as well. Whether it's the army or an international conglomerate, we have an expectation that you as a professional are going to develop yourself professionally. While we expect that, you can expect that we'll help you grow professionally, and you can also expect that we'll put you in an organization where you'll learn on the job. You'll learn by doing. We call that experiential learning.

The key here is to put your people through a variety of different on-the-job experiences as a way to make them as adaptable and resilient as possible.

In the army, especially with general officers, we intentionally pull people out of their comfort zone and throw them into something else whenever we have the chance. In fact, I would say I spent six out of my ten years as a general officer out of my comfort zone. When I was the chief of staff at Kosovo Force (KFOR), I was out of my comfort zone. When I was the operations officer for Southern Europe in Naples, Italy, I was out of my comfort zone. When I was the spokesman for the force in Iraq, I was *way* out of my comfort zone.

When I had a chance to become an assistant division commander, my superior, Division Commander Ben Griffin, said, "Hey, Rick, I can make you the assistant division commander for maneuver and you'd learn nothing because you already know all that stuff, so instead I'm going to make you the assistant division commander for support."

That type of career maneuvering in the army was purposeful. The point was that keeping me in one position, even one that I was good at, wouldn't give me a breadth of experience. The thought was that by causing me to move to a side of the division that I'd never been in before—to force me to move outside my comfort zone and experience something new—would make me a better division commander when I got my next promotion.

Later on, when I went to IMCOM and took over all the army installations worldwide, I was once again out of my comfort zone. It was 120,000 employees of whom only 2,000 were soldiers—the rest were dedicated civilians. That was a significant point of adaptation. I had to ask myself (and my mentors), "How do you take the mannerisms and techniques you used when you led soldiers and apply that to leading a civilian organization?" The answer was that I had to adapt. I had to learn on the job.

Now that I'm out of the army, I'm doing it again. I'm in an environment where I'm dealing with university personnel—a faculty—which is very different from what I did in the army with the department of army civilians. It's a different focus, a different temperament, a different prioritization. Getting through it and working within a new expectation structure—military vs. civilian vs. university faculty—is pure adaptation. And because of the experiential learning I've encountered along the way in my career, I've learned how to discern ways to effectively lead all three of these very different groups of people.

In the military, soldiers respond to orders. You tell 'em to go left, they go left. They don't argue the point. (At least that's the way it's supposed to work!)

When you're dealing with civilians, they'll listen to the order and then make a determination about whether they're going to do it. Even though they acknowledge you're the guy in charge, a lot of times they're going to listen and make up their own mind. So you have to be conscious of that, and as a result of that you have to tell your people not just what to do but *why they're doing it*. That's a major point of adaptation.

Soldiers want to be told what to do, and then they'll do it. Then they'll say, "If you get around to it, General, please tell us why we did it." But civilians? They want to know why they're doing it up front. They want it to make sense. They want to know that this isn't an exercise in futility before they get started. A lot of managers forget that—to their own peril. Then they're left wondering why their people aren't doing what they were told to do! Making this important adaptation when I got to IMCOM was a primary reason for going out on the road and visiting as many installations as I could during my two-year run. I had to get in front of those 120,000 workers and let them know the "whys" behind all of the changes and budget cuts the organization was going through.

In the academic world, on the other hand, I find myself dealing with a big "What's in it for me?" attitude. First of all, the academic research world has a major problem with stovepipes: Every college, every department is doing its own thing, and none of them are communicating with one another. It's a problem the United States military faces, and plenty of big corporations face as well.

Think about it this way: The army is a 1.1 million-person, $245 billion enterprise—just like Coca-Cola's an enterprise and Proctor & Gamble is an enterprise. If you run your enterprise as a stovepipe— every group doing its own thing—you're going to be much less efficient than if you cooperate across divisions and brands. The essence of an enterprise is: "Quit worrying about what's best for me, and start thinking about what's good for all of us."

When I ran the Services and Infrastructure Core Enterprise, an organization that was attempting to bridge the gaps between various services at our army installations, it wasn't about the three-star who ran the medical community, or the three-star who ran the corps of engineers, or the three-star who ran all the services. It was about, collectively, how do we approach our end-state in an efficient fashion using the enterprise approach? I've spent a lot of time talking to corporations about that, and they struggle with it. I've spent a lot of time talking with university presidents about it, too, saying, "We've got departments that aren't talking with one another and are concerned only with their departments and not what's best for the university as a whole, and we need to address that—because it's a cultural change."

The second problem I see in academia is the unbelievably inordinate use of the first-person pronoun. Among the staff at universities, everything is about "me." "I did this, this is mine, I'm not going to tell you about what I'm doing because I'm going to protect my intellectual property."

How, as a leader, can you get over a hurdle that big? Once again, my experiential learning has come into play. I've had to figure out that my role as a leader at a university isn't just to tell the faculty what we're doing and why we're doing it, but to tell them what's in it *for them.* What's the incentive for them to want to cooperate? That's especially true with tenured faculty. Even the president of a university will tell you that you can't tell tenured faculty what to do. I mean, the system says that if you've got tenure, you're safe. There's a tenure review process every six years or so, but I don't think anybody in the history of any university has ever been removed! So there couldn't be a more dysfunctional system, and a leader has to figure out how to work within that system—a system in which there's no real incentive to do anything different, where the attitude is, "This is what I'm going to do because I've been doing it this way so far, and the job pays pretty well, so why should I worry about doing anything different?"

Figuring out how to lead through any of those sorts of frameworks involves adaptation. It takes an ability to stand back, look at a population, and try to figure out, "How can I lead and manage these folks?"

The point I want to make here is that if you have a wide breadth of experiential learning behind you, you can adapt. If I could get what I wanted from our soldiers in the army and the Sunni population in Iraq, chances are I can get what I need in the university system. And if you've laid a foundation of adaptation and resiliency brought on by a broad range of experience, chances are you can get it done in whatever corporation or organization you're leading.

So ask yourself: Have you been in your comfort zone for too long? Is there something you can do to shake things up? Is there a move you could make that would challenge you in some way you've never been challenged before? Because every time you do that, you're going to grow stronger, and your ability to lead will grow stronger, too.

26

Do Less Better

Dealing with budget cuts is a lot like going to war.

Let me explain what I mean.

Carl von Clausewitz wrote a book called *On War*—a book that all military leaders have to read. It's required reading to this day despite the fact that Clausewitz was a Prussian soldier and philosopher who died back 1831. I've probably read it twenty times over the course of my military career. Everywhere you go they make you read that book because its thoughts and lessons apply to so much of what we still aspire to today.

One of the things Clausewitz talks about in *On War* is ends, ways, and means.

The "ends" refers to the end-state, or what you're trying to accomplish; the "means" are the resources you have to accomplish it; and the "ways" are the methods by which you're going to get it done.

When I took over IMCOM in my last two years in the army, the powers that be made one thing very clear: The ends were going to remain the same. We had 163 army installations worldwide, and it was our job at Installation Management Command—make that *my* job as the head of IMCOM—to provide our soldiers and their families with a quality of life commensurate with their quality of service. That's what we were tasked to accomplish, and that's what I *had* to do. No ifs, ands, or buts.

There was just one problem. We had a $20-billion-a-year budget at our disposal when I started my command, but as soon as I walked in the door I was told that by the end of those two years, our proposed budget would be cut back to $15 billion per year.

Can you imagine? "Don't change what you're doing. You need to deliver the same services you've been delivering. You just need to do it with potentially $5 billion less."

If that's not just about as daunting as going to war, I don't know what is. And if Clausewitz's words ever applied to a situation outside of war more directly than they did to this, I can't imagine what it would be.

To break it down in *On War* terms, ask yourself this question: If your ends are constant and your means are reduced, what do you have to do? The answer is: You have to modify your ways. Just as we did in Iraq in initiating the Sons of Iraq program, you have to change the way you're doing business. How? You can look for increases in effectiveness, increases in efficiency, different approaches—but whatever it is, you have to do it smartly so you'll still accomplish the same ends, even with significantly reduced means. That's what Clausewitz argues. And that's what we did at IMCOM. We worked to maintain that end state with billions in reduced resources—a reduction of 25 percent—and because of who I am and what I stand for, I saw to it that we didn't sacrifice our people to do it. I don't mean that we didn't trim the work force. We did. In the end, there was no choice. But we did even that in the most humane way possible, while giving those who would be forced to leave the means necessary to move on successfully. I'll talk more about how I did that momentarily, but what I'm saying here is that we accomplished our trims without overburdening the work force.

We accomplished our goals while still getting everybody home to their families for dinnertime.

If you know anything about me by now, you understand how important that was to me. Hopefully you're beginning to recognize how important it is to everything I hold dear, and to everything we should hold dear as Americans. Because budget cuts are happening. Everywhere. And I believe too many of those cuts are being made carelessly, sometimes recklessly, with only short-term gains at the heart of each panicked decision. That needs to stop. There's more than one way to skin a cat, folks, and I know for a fact that there's more than one way to trim the fat—no matter how much fat you've got to trim.

Five *billion* dollars is a lot of fat! Someone else could've come through the door slashing and burning everything in sight when faced with the cuts that were coming. Someone else might have taken resources away from everyone, and told everyone to just "ruck up." Another leader could have fired big chunks of the work force and told everyone else to make up for the work by working three times as hard—and if you've spent any time in corporate America, I'm sure you've seen that scenario time and time again. It seems to be the standard practice these days: Just make sure everyone works longer hours for less pay and reduced benefits, and tell them to suck it up!

I refused to do that.

Figuring out how to adapt the organization to those massive cuts without compromising my personal values and beliefs was absolutely critical. And that meant making those cuts while taking care of our most important resource: Our people.

Making Efficiency Efficient

I hate the phrase "Do more with less." That's code for abusing your work force. "Do more with less" implies, "I'm going to give you fewer resources, so you've just got to work harder." That, my friends, is absurd. It's the polar opposite of how we should be treating our people, and the antithesis of good business practice as far as I'm concerned.

I say, "Do less better."

"Do less better" means focus on what's important. Prioritize your tasks. Allocate your time and your resources. Resources are generally in three categories: people, time, and money. When companies get in a situation where they're facing reduced resources, what management automatically seems to fall back to is a position of making people work harder. And I think that is exactly wrong.

It's yet another case of "what managers do—not what *leaders* do." And we need more leaders.

Going back and forth between IMCOM's San Antonio headquarters and the Pentagon during this process, I picked up on a few things—mostly things that made me grateful that San Antonio is a long way from Washington.

The first thing I noticed was that when you talk about millions at the Pentagon, nobody cares. But talk about billions? I can guarantee you people will listen. Inside the Pentagon there were continual budget cuts. Every time you turned around you were losing some money. If you made a decision not to go to a meeting when budget was being discussed, you were going to lose part of your budget. In fact, there was a phrase in the Pentagon to describe this phenomenon: "If you're not at the table, you're on the menu."

Whenever you have budget cuts inside the Department of Defense, rather than looking at which program to cut or what headquarters we could do without, we would salami-slice everything. The so-called "easy way" was to just take 10 percent away from everybody rather than close something down.

That, candidly, is the wrong way to do business. All you're left with after making across-the-board cuts is no one having enough money to do what they need to do. Instead, why not make smart cuts and give certain areas of your organization—the right areas—the money they need to do what they do even better? Too often that thought fell on deaf ears.

Combine that with the fact that most people throughout the organization had no idea what cuts were coming, how deep those cuts would be, or how their departments would be affected each time a new set of cuts came down, and the whole thing just created waves of uneasiness and a work force that never knew where it stood. There's no better way to create an unstable organization than to keep your people in the dark.

My job, the way I saw it, was to eliminate any such nonsense at IMCOM.

My approach from day one was to communicate with subordinates all the time so they knew where I was coming from—and they knew what was coming. As I described previously, I traveled to my staff and talked to them directly. In person. I sent written communiqués all the time to tell my people what was happening and *why*. Remember, IMCOM had 120,000 employees when I started, of which only about 2,000 were military personnel. This was a predominantly civilian work force, the size of a Fortune 100 company. Civilians don't just follow orders. They need to understand those orders. They need to know where they stand. They want to feel connected to the decisions. So telling people about the situation was paramount.

My next step was to engage the staff in the decision-making process. I made the final decisions. Don't get me wrong, I wasn't about to turn IMCOM into some feel-good commune where decisions were made by raising hands around a fire while we all sang "Kumbaya." But I did appeal to the work force to share their ideas on how we could make cuts, given the hard, cold fact that cuts were going to happen.

IMCOM itself had become extremely bloated over the years. Think about this: The army had an $80 billion budget pre-9/11 that grew to $245 billion over ten years. Headquarters, size of forces, things people were doing that they no longer needed to do—you could see that everywhere. So my message was, "Okay, we're going to lose this money and we don't want to have to cut back on staff. You've all got families to feed and house payments to make. I want to make the reduction of the work force the very last option. With that in mind, help me see where we can do things differently and save a whole lot of time and money in the process."

That was the start of the Stamp Out Stupid campaign, which I described earlier—an effort that yielded about a hundred solid ideas from my staff. Ideas that I was able to turn into action.

The fact is, the Department of Defense had become expert at starting programs, but it was very poor at ending programs that had become unnecessary or redundant. Part of that was due to political pressures. I'd go to the Hill on a regular basis, called over by a member of Congress, and the conversation would always go like this: "General, we understand the budget cuts you're dealing with. We applaud the efficiencies you're pursuing, but we'd appreciate it if you'd pursue those cuts in somebody else's district."

That was all well and good. I'm glad they voiced their concerns. I was happy to listen. But the political concerns were not the most important concern to me. What was most important was protecting our people. So I'd leave the Hill and go back to work—aggressively working to cut through costly redundancies and unnecessary expenses regardless of what "district" they fell in.

One big area where I could make cuts was in our reliance on contractors. By definition, contractors cost a lot more than your old work force. IMCOM had a thousand people in its headquarters, and 543 of them were contractors. That was one place I immediately said, "Let's do less better. We're going to eliminate our reliance on contractors."

In the first year, they were migrated into other contracts elsewhere. There was great hue and cry, of course. The contractors felt they were entitled to those jobs and thought I was being the mean guy. We had to work through that, and it wasn't easy, but we ended up having a much smaller headquarters, and the headquarters itself was able to work more efficiently—protecting the army civilians in the process.

As an engaged leader—Managing by Walking Around rather than dictating any of this from some corner office—I'd see people working on things and I'd ask them, "Why are you doing that?"

"Because we've always done it that way" was a red flag for me. With massively reduced means, there is no excuse for doing things the way they've always been done unless they're the most efficient ways possible. One of the biggest red-flag areas I came across was reports. I was told that our headquarters required a total of 640-some-odd reports to be filed each year. That's 640-plus reports from 163 installations worldwide. That sounded like a lot.

How many of those reports actually make it to my in-box? I wondered.

Turns out only forty of those 640 reports ever made it to the decision maker!

"Why are we doing that?" I asked. "What good does it do? If the vast majority of reports result in no action, what's the point?"

You could've heard the crickets.

The fact was, many members of the work force relied on those reports to justify their existence. They gathered those numbers and made those reports. That was their job.

I decided to eliminate all of the meaningless reports. Reducing reports meant reducing the amount of work, and in some cases reducing the number of workers where it was truly justified.

Filling out reports for the sake of filling out reports is nothing but hole-digging. What's hole-digging? It's the sort of thing a leader witnesses when he walks by an employee and sees them working hard, breaking a sweat, digging a hole by the side of the road. "Good work," the leader says as he or she walks on by. The following day, the leader walks by and sees that employee hard at work again, only this time the employee is filling the hole back in. The point is, the employee is working hard, but he isn't accomplishing anything. The way I see it, there's a whole lot of hole-digging going on across America, and it simply needs to stop.

In my campaign to Stamp Out Stupid, I asked my staff to find me places where we were hole-digging at IMCOM, and to email me directly with their thoughts. When I went out on the road, visiting eighty-two of those installations during my two years, I would get up in front of our workers and demonstrate the hole-digging story with great theatrics to make it perfectly clear, so they would understand that I was eliminating reports (and therefore sometimes jobs) for good reason.

I wanted them to think for themselves, *Why* couldn't *we eliminate those reports? What would be lost?*

I wanted them to ask the question, "Is it good enough to keep doing something simply because everyone who came before did it a certain way?" And I wanted them to know that the answer is, "Absolutely not." In fact, that practice, that policy is the opposite of good. No one in your organization should be working with no progress. No one.

It was clear to me from commanding at Fort Stewart and Fort Hood that IMCOM potentially had too much overhead. Ten years prior to my arrival, there was no IMCOM. It was a new organization. By the time I got there, it was clearly bloated. In addition to IMCOM headquarters and our 163 installations, there were regional headquarters set up as go-betweens for the garrisons and IMCOM headquarters. A senior-executive civilian or a general officer led each of these regional headquarters. And each of those regional headquarters had become bloated with staffs of three hundred to four hundred people.

When I asked our staff to Stamp Out Stupid, almost uniformly they said, "We need to get rid of regional headquarters." In short, they were pass-through headquarters. Go-betweens. Just bloat smack dab in the middle of the organization.

Gee, I bet you haven't seen any of *that* in corporate America, have you? What about in other government organizations? Schools? Universities? You name it, and it's got bloat in the middle somewhere. It's as if the bloat of our organizations has grown right along with the average waistlines of the American public! It's like a symptom of years of excess. And it's not healthy.

I eliminated one regional headquarters right at the beginning of my command, and dropped IMCOM down from seven to four regional headquarters before I was through—with lots of gnashing of teeth in between.

Putting three to four hundred people out of a job is something that goes against my nature, of course. These are people with families and mortgages and college tuitions to pay for. It was imperative from the very beginning that we work hard to find these people jobs somewhere else. We gave them that latitude.

I learned a lot about downsizing from Reg Brack, chairman emeritus at Time, Inc. (the great magazine conglomerate headquartered in Manhattan). He's another mentor of mine who I've turned to for guidance from time to time, especially when struggling with these sorts of issues—having to let go of so many individuals whom I feel such a strong duty to protect, as I would my own children. His take, which I've come to embrace, is that when it comes to downsizing, you have to depersonalize it—but you also have to do it with compassion.

Even though you love your staff, when your organization no longer needs them, you've got to do away with them, but you've got to do it with compassion. Help them find a different job, get more education, move to a different place, whatever it may be. We tried to make it as painless as possible.

No matter how gently I tried to do it, there was a whole bunch of unhappy people out there because they'd always had these regional headquarters, and the idea that you could do away with those regions was unthinkable to them. But when all was said and done, when we went from seven headquarters to four, you couldn't tell the difference. The organization ran just as smoothly if not more smoothly, despite millions in cuts and the absence of all of those people. So it needed to be done. And making those hard decisions—that's what leaders have to do.

Stand Up for Your Decisions

The problem I see in many organizations is that nobody today wants to accept responsibility for tough decisions. I went to those regions and personally stood up in front of those three hundred or so people and said, "I'm going to deactivate this headquarters, here's the timeline, and here's what we're going to do to help you."

We found many of those employees work in other installations. We helped with job searches elsewhere. We provided every bit of assistance we could. And even so, people were mad at me.

The thing I found out the hard way is that generals are almost continuously under investigation for one thing or another. Unhappy employees make anonymous allegations against generals all the time. I suffered lots of that even though I was trying to do all of this in a kind and gentle fashion. We went above and beyond to help with moving people into new positions and new areas, but we still had a lot of unhappy people because they lost the job they had. It just comes with the territory, and I tried not to take it personally.

While all of this was going on, I was working to make the work-life balance better for every single employee in that 120,000-strong organization. "Do less better" was my never-ending mantra, as I refused to pile more work onto employees' plates to make up for any employees that we let go. In fact, I worked to take things off of their plates all the time. I refuse to abuse a work force, and when it comes right down to it, the only person who can determine what to take off anyone's plate is the leader. No one else is going to touch it because they don't want the leader getting mad about something not being done the way it's always been done. That's true no matter how many times you tell your staff otherwise. The leader has to be the one to step up and say, "We don't need to do that anymore. Focus on all of that other good work you're doing, and let's let that one thing go."

When you run a large business, half of your money is tied up in payroll, health insurance, and so forth, and it's up to you to trim from programs or services that won't harm those all-important areas. For IMCOM, that meant cutting some long-established programs. The army had billions invested in programs that had outlived their usefulness. It seemed like common sense to just about everyone to go ahead and cut those programs, but once again, politics came into play. If I tried to cut a long-standing program, chances are there was a government contract involved or a constituent of some member of Congress who was going to be affected. Suddenly I'd get called over the Hill to justify cutting a program in their district.

Escorted over to an office by a congressional liaison, I'd sit down and face a roomful of people who knew I was saying the truth: "We have a deficit and we *have* to do this."

But at the end of the day, they need votes. They need happy constituents. So they tried, even though I was resolute. Nothing ever changed in those offices other than the fact that they might be able to say to someone important to them, "I talked to the general in charge, and he heard me."

But I didn't change any decision based on trips to the Hill. I couldn't. Those outdated, no-longer-useful programs had to go. Remember, I had $5 billion to trim! And I wasn't going to trim anything that would affect the services that were important to our soldiers and their families. They were the people I was charged with caring for, not some congressman's constituents.

Of course, some people, no matter what you tell them, take it personally, and that's hard. The hardest thing I had to do during my two years at IMCOM was draw down the work force. In the end, we cut about three thousand positions under my watch. I did everything I could to do right by those people, given the unbelievably difficult circumstances. But I know a lot of those people resent me for it, and for a leader who cares, that's not easy.

I have to live with my decisions. I stand by my decisions. And I certainly have plenty of decisions that have weighed on my heart. As a leader, that's just inevitable.

Looking back at my time at IMCOM, I'm reminded that taking care of our soldiers and their families is the primary goal of that massive organization. Seeing to it that IMCOM operated efficiently and effectively in delivering on that mission no matter how much the budget was slashed was actually a way for me to honor those men and women in my work—along with every man and woman in uniform across all of our army installations around the globe.

So as tough as it was, I'm proud of what we were able to accomplish in those two years. I'm proud of the work force that helped me to Stamp Out Stupid. I'm proud of all of those employees who embraced the notion of "Do less better" while also embracing my desire to see them manage their time better and get home for dinner. And I'm proud of all of those men and women who moved on and made way for leaner times that were unavoidable. As much as they were the "casualties" or the "wounded" of this war in the form of budget cuts, I hope they know that they, too, made a difference—an important difference—in the lives of our soldiers and their families.

27

Transitioning

In the United States military, about two years prior to retirement, they ask general officers to take what's called a General Officer Transition Course. Like it or not, it really gets you thinking about the issues you're gonna face in retirement. You do that even before you have a definitive retirement date, when everyone knows you're long enough in the tooth that you *will* have to retire sometime. Then, once you have a definitive retirement date, they ask you to go through the course all over again. So we've got a pretty rigid approach about how to prepare generals to transition out of the military.

I embraced those courses for one very important reason: Going through them early gave Sarah and me lots of time to think about what we wanted to do after we got out of the army. (And make no mistake about it: A military spouse is very much *in* the military. It affects their lives just as deeply, if not more, than any soldier's or officer's.)

Pretty early on, she and I came up with the idea that we weren't ever going to use the word *retire*. We were simply going to use the word *transition* to mark our transitioning from one form of service into another. The more I thought about it, the more I made up my mind that whatever I did once I left the army, it was going to be meaningful and substantive work around people with shared values.

I have to say, it's nice to have that kind of freedom: To truly choose what it is you want to do. We all have that choice. Everything in life is a choice, isn't it? But we don't always exercise that right to choose, especially when it comes to career. There are just too many pressures on us when we're young, and especially when we're married with children—pressures that lead us to sometimes make choices that are rushed and, let's face it, aren't always ideal. Preparing to transition out of the military gave me the opportunity and time to properly consider my options, and to weigh those options against what truly was most important to me.

They coach you in the military about the four variables in the basic career equation—the job itself, the pay, the location, and the proximity to friends and family—and it's up to you to figure out how you want to weigh those variables. What's most important to you? In Sarah's and my transition, what was most important to us was to remain in the Texas area, to be close to our family and friends, and then to have meaningful, substantive work. We didn't spend a whole lot of time talking about how much money I wanted to make; that just wasn't at the top of either of our priority lists.

On November 17, 2011, I changed command, and on the first of January 2012, I officially entered the retired rolls of the United States military.

My first command decision in "transition" was to spend four months doing nothing but spending time with Sarah and my family. We spent time with my son, Lucas, who's an entrepreneur now right in our home state of Texas, and we traveled to California to see my daughter, Susan, who's an actress now, and we traveled to Ohio to see my dad, and so forth. It was a wonderful gift not to truncate our vacation time to hurry back for some pressing matter or, God forbid, another deployment. It felt good to operate on *my* time instead of military time.

Leaving the army as a three-star lieutenant general, I found plenty of doors open to me in the civilian world. About twelve companies wanted me to consult for them. I had pro bono opportunities at a good number of nonprofits that wanted my help. And I had a few companies that wanted me to work for them full time, running parts of their organizations.

In the end, I boiled it down to what made the most sense for me and my family, and what best lined up with my goals for the future. I would consult with three companies. I would make speeches around the world about leadership. I would write this book. And I would take advantage of the chance to run the University of Texas at Arlington Research Institute, with a goal of using advanced technology to help humanity. That desire can be traced all the way back to my time at MIT, later endorsed by my desire to be in charge of something, and bolstered by my experiences on the battlefield. After all, I still keep that stack of laminated pictures on my desk, commemorating those men who died on my watch in Iraq. Many of them might have lived had we used unmanned vehicles and other technology in their place on the battlefield.

All of it is meaningful and substantive work around people with shared values.

I used that desire as my lens for what I wanted to pursue, and that is exactly what I am pursuing.

I began "working" again on April 2, 2012.

After thirty-five years in the military, it seems like it would be hard to adjust to civilian life, right? Wrong! It actually couldn't be better. The only problem is that Sarah and I have a serious facial affliction: We can't stop smiling!

I loved being in the army, but I love being out of the army, too. It's worked out well. Perhaps if I had devoted my life only to my profession, I'd have had unbelievable fears and worries that I'd walk out of the military and have nothing. But I prioritized my life way back in the 1980s: My relationship with God came first, my relationship with my family came second, and my profession always, always came third.

Think about this: In the military, when you assume command, there's a big parade. You stand on a platform and people give speeches, and when the parade is over, this giant group of soldiers do what's called a pass and review: they turn right face, then left face, then pass in front of the reviewing stand so the new commander can observe this fine group he'll be leading for the next two years. When all of those soldiers finally walk away, the new commander walks away with them. It's a wonderful ceremony, full of symbolism and honor and tradition.

Two years later, there's an identical parade—only this time with a new commander. The speeches are all about saying good-bye to you and welcoming this new commander. The pass and review is for this new commander. And when the soldiers walk away, that new commander walks away with them, and you're left standing there on the podium with your family.

If you sacrificed spending time with your family during those two years of command, guess what? You're standing there all by yourself. And then what?

You were the big man on campus for two years. You commanded that unit. You had hundreds of guys saluting you everywhere you went. But now what? What are you? The fact is, no matter what your position, you are always the husband of your wife and the father of your children, and *that's* what's important. Even the president of the United States is only president for four years, eight if he's lucky. What happens when those years in the White House are over? He is always the husband and always the father.

At the end of the parade that was my career—which was thirty-five years of active duty—when the army walked away, I was still standing on that platform with my family. We simply transitioned from army life into another form of life. When I walked out of the military I had zero concerns that I would be entering civilian life as a lonely man, because I had dedicated time to Sarah and the kids.

A lot of folks might have fears or worries as they prepare to head into retirement from any profession. But candidly, because I stayed true to my beliefs and priorities, I didn't have any. My identity was never, "I'm the general." My identity was, "I'm Sarah's husband and the father of Susan and Lucas." Staying true to that made this whole transition easy, because I maintained my identity after I took off the uniform.

I won't say I didn't have concerns. One big tangential concern was that I might lose my ability to touch the lives of soldiers, personally, on a daily basis. Over thirty-five years I had developed this passion for soldiers and their families, and I was worried I might lose the ability to spend time with them and work for their benefit. But I soon found that was an unnecessary concern. I'm still working with soldiers. There's a large ROTC battalion at U.T. Arlington, and I'm involved in training the cadets. I can continue that sort of work for the rest of my life, or at least as long as I can walk, if I so choose. Even out of the military, I can still reach out to soldiers as much as I want to. So it's not a problem.

I think there are always ways to stay involved in something you love.

Do What Makes You Happy, and Your Life Will Be Fulfilled

My mantra in my life has been to touch lives and make a difference, so I've devoted a lot of energy since my retirement to leadership development, and sharing my experiences of leading in difficult circumstances to bodies large and small, including in corporate America and the nonprofit world. I'm continuously amazed at how the lessons I've learned in my military career apply so aptly to so many organizations and to so many people from so many walks of life.

Sure, I retired as required. But my ability to touch lives and to "lead" remains.

As I've said before, I achieved my highest goal in the army back in 1993. Everything after that was gravy. So retiring wasn't a letdown. It was just a next step.

People ask me all the time, "After thirty-five years in the army, what's your favorite memory?" and "Where'd you make the most difference?"

I have to say, my favorite time was just after I accomplished my career goal: When I became a battalion commander and served as a lieutenant colonel from 1993 to 1995. Why? I think it's because for the first time, I was really in charge and really had the ability to affect the lives of soldiers and their families on a broad yet still-personal level. There I was heading up the First Battalion of Eighth Cavalry, 450 soldiers and their families, and the army gave me all the trust and confidence and opportunity I needed to make a difference in those people's lives. I was there every day with those soldiers and their families—not in some office or headquarters somewhere, but right there with them. Day and night. It was a wonderful time. Sarah and I cherished every moment of every day.

As for where I made the biggest difference? That's easy: Leading Task Force Marne in the surge. Taking those 25,000 soldiers into the Triangle of Death and turning it into the Triangle of Life in fifteen months—that truly was the culmination of nearly everything I had worked toward and everything I wanted to be as a leader in the army. Transitioning that team from combat operations to rebuilding has to be just about the most extreme example of adaptation "in action" that I can imagine. It was a case of saving lives—countless lives, in fact, on all sides—while changing lives for the better. It was a case of setting an example for our soldiers, and the army as a whole, as to just how broad and adaptable we could be as a force for change in the modern world. And I hope it serves as an example to the world.

I stand back in awe of what we were able to accomplish in that harsh environment, in the middle of that seemingly impossible situation.

Of course, the funny thing is that now I don't spend a whole bunch of time sitting around thinking about it. In fact, I don't spend a whole lot of time thinking about the army, period. I find myself so active in philanthropy, research, and making presentations that I can't remember a single moment in the last few months when I found myself sitting around thinking about the army except when I've been working on this book. That's pretty amazing considering it's just about all I thought about for thirty-five years. Heck, thirty-nine years when you count West Point!

The only explanation I have for that ability to let it go, and for my ability to move on, is that it comes as a direct result of "living my dash." It's a direct result of staying true to my priorities in life. It's a direct result of walking the walk and practicing what I preach. I've been able to adapt to life outside the army just as easily as I adapted to changes within it because I've always focused on what it takes to be a resilient person and a resilient leader, and I've focused on seeing the opportunities in this career transition rather than the obstacles that might have seemed so daunting to someone else in my position.

It took a lifetime of lessons and a litany of experience to reach this comfort level, of course, and today I'm making the most of everything I've learned by sharing my passion for leadership wherever I can. It's my great hope that some of these lessons will have an impact on your life and career, and that in time you'll share the positive results of your own leadership lessons with others, wherever you can.

After all, we're in this together. And it's up to us leaders to help make sure that we all move forward, through whatever obstacles we face—with strength, with grace, with dignity, and with honor.

In the end, it's up to leaders to lead. And it's up to you to decide what kind of a leader you want to be.

It's your choice. It's your decision.

But if you're gonna be a leader, I hope that you always remember: The very future of our businesses, our churches, our schools, our governments, our country, and especially our people depends on one thing: *you.*

I pray that you make the right choices. I pray that you build a solid foundation on which to stand, and then stand on that foundation firmly. I pray that you set your priorities in life, and that you always, always put your people first. Because the more of us who do that, the better off we're all going to be.

I thank you for taking the time to read this book. May God bless you and your family in all of your future endeavors.

Now . . .

Get out there and lead.

Appendix 1

Lynch's Leadership Principles

1. Focus on opportunities, not obstacles.
   "It can be done!"
2. Have fun!
   "If the boss ain't happy, ain't nobody happy!"
3. Achieve a work-life balance.
   "How are you living your dash?"
4. Decide when to decide.
   "Take the time to think!"
5. Look down, not up.
   "People don't care how much you know until they know how much you care!"
6. Be a mentor.
   "You must be accessible, you must listen, and you must truly care!"
7. Engaged leadership is important.
   "Love your subordinates like you love your own children!"
8. Be demanding but not demeaning.
   "Everyone must perform to his or her full potential."
9. Always celebrate diversity.
   "Don't surround yourself with people like you!"

Appendix 2

Lynch's Go-To Scriptures

John 15:13
Greater love has no one than this: to lay down one's life for one's friends.

Isaiah 6:8
Then I heard the voice of the Lord saying, "Whom shall I send? And who will go for us?" And I said, "Here am I. Send me!"

Matthew 25:21
His master replied, "Well done, good and faithful servant! You have been faithful with a few things; I will put you in charge of many things. Come and share your master's happiness!"

1 Chronicles 4:10 (The Prayer of Jabez)
Jabez cried out to the God of Israel, "Oh, that you would bless me and enlarge my territory! Let your hand be with me, and keep me from harm so that I will be free from pain." And God granted his request.

Joshua 1:8
Keep this Book of the Law always on your lips; meditate on it day and night, so that you may be careful to do everything written in it. Then you will be prosperous and successful.

Psalm 119:11
I have hidden your word in my heart that I might not sin against you.

Romans 3:23
For all have sinned and fall short of the glory of God.

Romans 5:3–4
Not only so, but we also glory in our sufferings, because we know that suffering produces perseverance; perseverance, character; and character, hope.

Romans 8:31
What, then, shall we say in response to these things? If God is for us, who can be against us?

Colossians 3:5–12
Put to death, therefore, whatever belongs to your earthly nature: sexual immorality, impurity, lust, evil desires and greed, which is idolatry. Because of these, the wrath of God is coming. You used to walk in these ways, in the life you once lived. But now you must also rid yourselves of all such things as these: anger, rage, malice, slander, and filthy language from your lips. Do not lie to each other, since you have taken off your old self with its practices and have put on the new self, which is being renewed in knowledge in the image of its Creator. Here there is no Gentile or Jew, circumcised or uncircumcised, barbarian, Scythian, slave or free, but Christ is all, and is in all. Therefore, as God's chosen people, holy and dearly loved, clothe yourselves with compassion, kindness, humility, gentleness and patience.

2 Timothy 3:16
All Scripture is God-breathed and is useful for teaching, rebuking, correcting and training in righteousness.

2 Timothy 4:7
I have fought the good fight, I have finished the race, I have kept the faith.

1 John 1:8–10

If we claim to be without sin, we deceive ourselves and the truth is not in us. If we confess our sins, he is faithful and just and will forgive us our sins and purify us from all unrighteousness. If we claim we have not sinned, we make him out to be a liar and his word is not in us.

Philippians 4:6–7

Do not be anxious about anything, but in every situation, by prayer and petition, with thanksgiving, present your requests to God. And the peace of God, which transcends all understanding, will guard your hearts and your minds in Christ Jesus.

Matthew 5:16

In the same way, let your light shine before others, that they may see your good deeds and glorify your Father in heaven.

Acknowledgments

This book would not have been possible without a lot of love, guidance, and friendship through the years, and while many of those who helped me along the way are mentioned in the pages of this book already, I'd like to take a moment here to salute a few of them.

First of all, I'd like to thank the amazing soldiers with whom I've had the privilege to serve. They are the real heroes of our nation. I am humbled to be in their presence. Thanks as well to the mentors who showed me the way, listened to my concerns and questions, and always provided wise counsel (even though sometimes I chose to ignore it).

Thanks to my family—my wife, Sarah, and our children, Susan and Lucas—for their "acceptance" of the military lifestyle and the too-numerous moves that came along with it. To my mom and dad, for establishing in me a work ethic that helped me through all the stages of my life. And to the friends who were always by my side and never gave up on me.

I want to express my sincere thanks to Mark Dagostino, my collaborator on this project. His passion and professionalism were truly the engine that made this book possible. It would have been impossible for me to get this book into the hands of the reader without his tireless efforts and dedication. I enjoyed every moment I spent with Mark on this effort.

Thank you to my agent, Joel Kneedler, for his dedication and perseverance as he took me by the hand and showed me the way to publication. Thanks as well to my editor, Jon Wilcox, and to all the folks at Baker Books for their professionalism, courtesy, and relentless focus on mission accomplishment.

And finally to God, who gave me the strength, courage, and wisdom to always attempt to do the right thing, even though I fell short of the mark on many occasions. To Him goes all the glory.

LT. GEN. (RET.) RICK LYNCH has commanded at all levels of the Army, from company (100 soldiers) to corps (65,000 soldiers) to commander of all U.S. Army installations (120,000 civilian employees and soldiers worldwide). He spent a total of over thirty months in Iraq, including fifteen months as one of the leaders of the 2007 surge, and is now executive director of the University of Texas at Arlington Research Institute. He and his wife of thirty years, Sarah, live in Texas.

MARK DAGOSTINO is a *New York Times* bestselling coauthor and former senior writer for *People* magazine. He wrote *Courage to Stand* with Minnesota Governor Tim Pawlenty, and is the coauthor of *Rudy: My Story* with Notre Dame legend Daniel "Rudy" Ruettiger. He lives in New Hampshire.